Transfer paper, white and grey
Water basin
Wood filler
Wood glue

T5-CQB-576

BRUSHES

I use a very limited selection of brushes. The following list and their uses may help you to paint the projects throughout this book.

ROYAL® & LANGNICKEL

Combo™ Series 3030 Fan: #3

A combination of synthetic and natural hairs used to soften and even brush strokes on larger areas of background.

Combo™ Series 3070 Glaze/wash: 1/2", 3/4" and 1"

A mix of synthetic and natural hair used for basecoating wood projects, moistening larger areas with retarder and applying background washes of color (for example, skies and the wood color on the "Christmas Carolers" project).

Pure Red Sable Series 1250 Round: #1, #3 and #5

A natural hair brush used for general painting techniques. Use the #1 as a liner. Natural hair brushes give a more casual watercolor appearance.

Royal Sable™ Series 5005 Short Round: #6

A natural hair brush used to stipple foliage.

Royal Sable™ Series 5020 Filbert: #4, #6 and #8

A natural hair brush used dry as a mop to soften and lighten areas of wet paint; also used for drybrushing.

Royal Sable™ Series 5060 Angular: 1/4"

A natural hair brush used to stipple the needles of the evergreen boughs on wreath and door garlands of the "Christmas Carolers" project. This brush improves as it becomes older and fluffs slightly.

Sunburst™ Series 2010 Bright (Flat): #8

A synthetic hair brush used for sideloading and floating colors. Creates a sharp edge that graduates away to nothing.

EVELENA So lovely to paint with you. Hugs Jen.

Sources

Ornaments and "Christmas Carolers" triptych
Philip Sykes
P. O. Box 6313
Panama City, FL 32404-0313
PH: (850) 871-3778

Candleholder and all small wooden objects
Casey's Wood Products, Inc.
P. O. Box 365
Wiscasset, ME 04578
PH: (800) 452-2739 for catalog
Web site: www.caseyswood.com

Brushes and "Christmas Bowl"
Stonebridge Collection
In the US:
107 Court Street, #255
Watertown, NY 13601
PH: (800) ART-TOLE
Web site: www.4packets.com

In Canada:
2 Mill Street, R.R. #4
Pakenham, ON K0A 2X0

Brushes
Stan Brown Arts and Crafts
13435 NE Whitaker Way
Portland, OR 97230
PH: (503) 257-0559
Web site: www.stanbrownartsandcrafts.com

"Christmas Ornament Box" 9" x 6-1/4" x 5-1/2" ball foot
Lancaster trunk
Walnut Hollow Farm, Inc.
1409 State Road 23
Dodgeville, WI 53533-2112
PH: (800) 395-5995

Candleholder and "Christmas Bowl"
Viking Woodcrafts, Inc.
1317 8th Street S.E.
Waseca, MN 56093
PH: (800) 328-0116   FAX: (507) 835-3895
Web site: www.vikingwoodcrafts.com

General Notes

BASECOATING

The first coat of paint applied to the wooden surface. Most of the projects featured in this book are basecoated with Jo Sonja's Background Colours Soft White mixed with Jo Sonja's Clear Glaze Medium (2:1). By mixing your paint with the clear glaze medium, you can achieve an application of both color and sealer in one step. When the first coat is dry, lightly sand and gently brush off sanding dust, then apply a second coat.

TRACING AND TRANSFERRING YOUR DESIGN

Cover the design pattern with a sheet of tracing paper and secure in place using a small square of masking tape. Using a fine tip pen or a 2B pencil, trace the basic outlines of the design. Position the traced design on your surface, using the masking tape to hold it in place. Slide the transfer paper

(Continued on Page 5)

Christmas Carolers Worksheet

Holly and Pine Boughs

Garden Lantern and Ivy

Boy Caroler and Scarf

General Notes
(Continued from Page 3)

between the tracing paper and surface, coated side down. Use white transfer paper for darker backgrounds and grey graphite for lighter backgrounds. Using the fine end of your stylus and very little pressure, trace over the traced design to transfer to your surface.

ART MASKING FLUID

Using art masking fluid is a wonderful way to give your project a watercolor appearance. Always apply soap to your old round brush before using masking fluid as this helps when cleaning your brush. Be very precise when applying the masking fluid. Mask foreground areas prior to painting background areas. Apply a good coverage to the design areas to keep them clear of the background wash. Allow masking fluid to dry or use a hair dryer on a medium setting. When background wash is dry, use your finger to roll away the masking fluid when ready to paint each individual item or a specific area.

DRYBRUSHING

Pick up the color on the dry brush. Tap off the excess paint onto a paper towel and gently brush color onto the specified area. This gives a textured appearance.

FLOATING COLOR

To apply highlighting and shading colors, dress a flat brush in Jo Sonja's Magic Mix and pick up (sideload) a little color on the corner of the brush. Blend the brush on your palette to ease the color through the brush hairs; the color should gradually fade to nothing before it reaches the opposite side of the brush.

SOFTENING COLOR

Basecoating a section of your design will achieve a fairly even distribution of color pigment. To lighten areas, use a dry

Royal Sable filbert and gently pat the area to soften the color. During this process, keep wiping the brush with a paper towel to keep the brush clean. Dry. The natural hair brush will absorb moisture more readily than the synthetic variety.

TINTING

Almost everything I paint gets a final tint of one color or another. Moisten the area to be tinted with your choice of medium. Water has the quickest drying time. Water + retarder (1:1) gives you more open time and pure retarder has the longest open time. When choosing a tinting color, use the more transparent colors. Thin the tinting color with the medium used to dampen the surface.

WASH

Color can be washed onto an area dampened with water or Jo Sonja's Retarder Medium to give a delicate transparent effect and to facilitate blending color. Moisten area, then use a large wash brush to add color. When using water, it is necessary to work quickly as the water dries quickly. Use retarder as the base when you need more time to blend your color.

FINISHING YOUR PIECE

Allow your painting to dry for 24 hours. Using water-based acrylic varnish (matte, satin or a (1:1) mix), apply at least two coats and allow drying time between coats. For heavily used surfaces, I recommend at least four coats. Allow the varnish to dry overnight.

Beeswax polish is used as the final step in completing some painted projects. *NOTE: Be sure to purchase turpentine-free beeswax polish or the turpentine in the polish will be harmful to your painted piece.* Apply the polish with a soft, lint-free cloth and buff to give a lovely protected finish.

Christmas Carolers Worksheet

Worksheet on Page 4

Please refer to General Notes for art masking fluid application and apply as shown on the worksheet. Dry and proceed with the various backgrounds shown. Please note that worksheet colors may vary from the project.

HOLLY AND PINE BOUGHS

1. Using an old, fluffed-out 1/4" angular brush loaded with *Teal Green*, stipple the foliage working from the tip of the bough. Upon completion, remove the masking from protected areas.

2. Basecoat the holly leaves with *Green Oxide*, the berries with *Naples Yellow Hue*, and the main branch with retarder-thinned *Raw Sienna + Raw Umber + Paynes Grey (2:1: touch)*.

In the same manner as in step 1, lighten the pine boughs by stippling with *Storm Blue + Warm White (1:1)*. Vary this mix.

3. Moisten the holly leaves with retarder, then shade the underside of each vein area and where one leaf overlaps another with *Green Oxide + Paynes Grey (2:1)*. While the surface is still moist, lighten one side of each leaf with *Yellow Light*.

Using your flat brush dressed with *Magic Mix* and sideloaded with *Red Earth*, float "C" strokes on opposite sides of each berry. Using a liner brush, dot the seed end with *Paynes Grey + Purple Madder (1: touch)*.

Using your flat brush dressed with *Magic Mix*, float shading on the boughs under the holly leaves with *Paynes Grey*.

(Continued on Page 6)

6

Christmas Carolers Worksheet

(Continued from Page 5)

Using the *step 2 branch color* and a liner brush, basecoat the thinner twigs and reinforce darker areas of the main branch.

4. Shade the berries with *Red Earth + Purple Madder (1:1)*. Dot a *Warm White* highlight on the lighter berries. Using liner brush, add *Warm White* to the holly leaf veins and the lighter edges. Strengthen the darker edges of the leaves with *Green Oxide + Paynes Grey (1:1)*. On a retarder-moistened surface, tint the holly leaves with *Aqua* near shaded areas and *Brilliant Green* as shown. Dry the leaves. Drybrush some *Warm White* highlights on the leaves.

Using your liner brush and *Warm White*, highlight the branch and twigs, and dot the lighter tips of the pine boughs.

With the same brush, paint the main branch of each pine bough with a broken line using *step 2 branch color*.

Using your round brush and water-thinned *Paynes Grey*, paint the shadows on the background. This color needs to be thinned considerably. Practice a little before proceeding on your design surface.

GARDEN LANTERN AND IVY

1. Remove mask when instructed to paint each of the masked areas. Using a liner brush, basecoat smaller branches *Warm White*.

2. Basecoat the branches, candleholder and post with *Nimbus Grey + Raw Sienna + Paynes Grey (1:1: touch)*. Paint candle through to completion in this step. Using a flat brush and *Raw Sienna + Paynes Grey (1: tiny touch)*, lightly shade the candle. Using the *shade color + Paynes Grey (1: touch)*, paint under the candle drips. Highlight the candle and drips with *Warm White*. Using liner brush, paint the frame section behind the candle flame with *Paynes Grey + Raw Umber (1:1)*. Dry. Paint the flame with thinned *Warm White*. Dry.

Tint the flame with *Vermilion + Yellow Light (2:1)*. Using a liner brush and the lantern frame mix, paint the candlewick.

Basecoat the ivy leaves with *Green Oxide*.

3. Shade the branches, candleholder and post with *Raw Umber + Paynes Grey (1: touch)*. Using the liner brush, paint the remaining lantern frame with *Paynes Grey + Raw Umber (1:1)*.

Shade the ivy leaves with *Green Oxide + Paynes Grey (1:1)*. Using a liner brush, paint the ivy vine with *Raw Sienna + Raw Umber + Paynes Grey (2:1: touch)*.

4. Using a liner or round brush for larger areas, drybrush *Warm White* to highlight the lantern, branch, candleholder, post and ivy leaves. Tint the drybrushed areas of the ivy leaves with *Yellow Light* to give a glow. Tint with *Aqua* near the shaded areas. Using a liner brush, paint *Warm White* on the veins and vines plus the lighter leaf edges.

To paint the glass panels, first moisten the surface with retarder. Thin your *Warm White* with retarder, then paint the glass to give it a thin streaked appearance. Drybrush the rays of light with *Warm White + Yellow Light (2:1)*. Shade the post under the lamp and ivy with water-thinned *Paynes Grey*.

BOY CAROLER

1. Basecoat the boy's entire head with *Skin Tone Base + Warm White (4:1)*. Dry. Repeat this step to give you a more even coverage.

Paint the eyes with *Sapphire*. Moisten the face with retarder and shade with *Burnt Sienna + Raw Sienna (1: touch)*; use a dry brush to soften the color. Basecoat the inside of the mouth with *Red Earth + Skin Tone Base (1:1)*.

2. While the surface is still moist, lighten the nose, chin, around eyes, below the eyebrows, and ear with *Warm White*; use a dry brush to soften appearance. Dry. Paint the pupils with *Paynes Grey*. Moisten the entire face and hair with retarder. Basecoat the hair with *Smoked Pearl + Raw Sienna (1: touch)*. Blush the cheeks and lower tip of the nose with *Red Earth + Skin Tone Base (1:1)*; use a dry brush to soften and blend the color.

3. To build up the eyes, paint *Warm White* in the lower corners of each eyeball. Dot tiny *Warm White* highlights on the pupils and irises to give a sparkle. Using a liner brush and *step 2 cheek color*, paint the lips. Moistened hair area with retarder, then shade with *Raw Sienna + Raw Umber (1: touch)*. With *step 2 hair color* and a liner brush, apply hair strands to soften the appearance, followed by touches of *Warm White*.

4. Additional shading under the hairline, at the side of the left eye, neck, and the right inside of the mouth is completed with very thin *Ultramarine Blue + Burnt Sienna (2:1)*. Using a liner brush and *step 1 shade color*, detail the eyebrows, eyelashes and around the nose area. Using same brush, highlight eyelashes, lips and hair strands with *Warm White*. Dry.

Moisten the cheeks and hair areas with retarder, then tint the lower outer cheek edges with *Amethyst*. Soften the color to blend onto the cheeks. Using *Yellow Light*, tint the hair that catches the lamp glow. Let dry, then drybrush *Warm White* to highlight the hair and face. At this time, evaluate your facial shading. To darken areas, moisten with retarder and shade with *step 1 shade color*.

SCARF

1. On a retarder-moistened surface, basecoat with *Nimbus Grey + Raw Umber (1: touch)*; stipple to give it a more wooly appearance. Dry.

2. Using a flat brush moistened with *Magic Mix* and side-loaded with *Nimbus Grey + Paynes Grey (1:1)*, float irregular stripes on the scarf.

3. Using a flat brush moistened with *Magic Mix*, float shading on the scarf folds with *Nimbus Grey + Raw Umber + Paynes Grey (1:1: touch)*.

4. Drybrush highlights with *Warm White*. On a retarder-moistened surface, tint the lamp glow on the scarf with *Yellow Light*.

Christmas Carolers
Triptych and Candleholder
Color Photo on Page 23

PALETTE

JO SONJA'S ARTISTS' COLOURS

Amethyst (Triptych)	Red Earth
Aqua	Red Violet
Brilliant Green	Sapphire (Triptych)
Burnt Sienna (Triptych)	Skin Tone Base (Triptych)
Celadon (Triptych)	Smoked Pearl (Triptych)
Green Oxide	Storm Blue
Naples Yellow Hue	Teal Green
Nimbus Grey (Triptych)	Turners Yellow (Triptych)
Paynes Grey	Ultramarine Blue
Purple Madder	Vermilion
Raw Sienna	Warm White
Raw Umber	Yellow Light

JO SONJA'S BACKGROUND COLOURS
Soft White

JO SONJA'S METALLIC COLOURS
Pale Gold

ADDITIONAL MATERIALS

Art masking fluid
Candleholder, 6-1/2" x 2-1/2"
Old toothbrush (Triptych)
Rubbing alcohol, isopropyl (Triptych)
Triptych, 14" x 17-1/4"

BACKGROUND PREPARATION

Please refer to "Basecoating," "Tracing and Transferring Your Design" and "Art Masking Fluid" at the front of the book.

Basecoat the triptych and candleholder with two coats of *Soft White + Clear Glaze Medium (2:1)*. Dry and lightly sand between coats. When dry, lightly transfer only the basic design lines.

Using art masking fluid, mask holly leaves, gingerbread basket and gingerbread men, stocking, tree trunk and larger branches, owl, lantern post, ivy leaves, lantern candle and candleholder, cat and group of carolers. Remove the masking when you are ready to paint that design element.

PAINTING YOUR DESIGN

Triptych

SKY

NOTE: When painting the sky colors, include the area behind the dark green foliage.

1. Moisten the entire sky area with retarder. Paint from the top of the door opening downwards with retarder-thinned *Storm Blue*. Soften brush strokes with your fan brush. Dry.

2. Moisten the sky area again with retarder and darken the top with *Paynes Grey*. Lighten the horizon with retarder-thinned *Aqua*. Soften the color with your fan brush. Dry.

3. Using the step 1 method, add a touch of *Red Violet* to the top-right corner of the sky.

PATHWAY

1. Moisten the pathway with retarder. Basecoat the pathway with retarder-thinned *Smoked Pearl + Nimbus Grey + Raw Sienna (2:2:1)*. On the still wet area, fleck the path with rubbing alcohol, using an old toothbrush, to give it an irregular appearance. Dry.

2. Moisten the pathway with retarder and paint it with a retarder-thinned *Raw Sienna + Paynes Grey (4:1)*. Even out your brush strokes with your fan brush, then fleck the area with rubbing alcohol. Dry.

MOSS ON THE PATHWAY AND WOODEN POST

1. *NOTE: Paint moss on post after painting the post.* Moisten the moss areas with retarder. Stipple clumps of moss with *Teal Green*. While areas are still moist, stipple *Green Oxide* to lighten, then gently stipple *Yellow Light* and, finally, a touch of *Warm White*. Dry.

2. On a retarder-moistened surface, shade the pathway below the children and the moss with *Paynes Grey*.

FOLIAGE

CHRISTMAS TREE (left side)

1. On a retarder-moistened surface, stipple *Teal Green* foliage, allowing the sky to penetrate through the branches. While still moist, stipple *Teal Green + Paynes Grey (2:1)* to shade the left side. Lighten the branch tips by stippling with the *step 1 pathway color*. Dry.

2. Using your flat brush dressed with *Magic Mix* and side-loaded with the *shading color*, shade between the branches with "V"-shaped brush strokes.

3. Using a liner brush, lightly paint visible branches with *Raw Umber + Paynes Grey (1: touch)*. Stipple touches of *Warm White* to highlight foliage.

4. Tint the white areas with *Yellow Light* stippling.

SHRUBS TO RIGHT AND BELOW LAMP

1. Stipple the shrubs with the same colors as the Christmas tree; the shrubs are more rounded in appearance. Add a touch of *Green Oxide* to the foreground shrub to give it a lighter appearance and stipple *Warm White* to highlight.

2. Tint the lighter areas with *Yellow Light* and tint near the shaded areas *Aqua*.

(Continued on Page 8)

Christmas Carolers

(Continued from Page 7)

JUNIPERS (left of the lantern post and behind the wooden post)

1. On a retarder-moistened surface, paint the trees thinned *Teal Green*. Dry.

2. With a flat brush dressed with *Magic Mix* and sideloaded with *Teal Green*, separate the branches using irregular brush strokes and the chisel edge of the brush. Stipple tiny touches of *Warm White* to highlight and *Yellow Light* in lighter areas, then tint with *Aqua*.

TREE TRUNK AND BRANCHES, LANTERN POST AND WOODEN POST

1. Using a liner brush, undercoat smaller branches with *Warm White*.

2. Basecoat all branches and wood areas with *Nimbus Grey + Raw Umber + Paynes Grey (1:1: touch)*. Shade with *Raw Umber + Paynes Grey (1: touch)*. Highlight with *Warm White*; drybrush the larger wood areas and use a liner brush to highlight the thinner branches.

IVY

1. Moisten areas behind the ivy leaves on sides of design with retarder, then darken with *Teal Green + Payne's Grey (1: touch)*. Dry.

2. Remove the masked areas on the ivy leaves only.

3. Refer to the Garden Lantern and Ivy section of the color worksheet to paint the ivy leaves.

GARDEN LANTERN

Refer to the Garden Lantern and Ivy section of the color worksheet.

CHRISTMAS CAROLERS

RED CLOTHING

1. On a retarder-moistened surface, basecoat the jacket and coat with *Red Earth*. Soften the color with a dry brush to enhance the lighter and darker areas. Dry.

2. On a retarder-moistened surface, shade with *Red Earth + Purple Madder (1:1)*. Dry.

3. Using a flat brush dressed with *Magic Mix*, shade the deeper areas with *Purple Madder*.

4. Using a liner brush, basecoat buttons with *Purple Madder*. With the same brush, add decorative stitching, buttonholes and fabric folds with *Red Earth + Purple Madder (1:1)*.

5. Drybrush *Warm White* to highlight the jacket and coat. Using a liner brush, highlight the buttons and paint the thread with *Warm White*.

6. Tint the darker areas with *Red Violet*.

    NOTE: Using the same colors as clothing, paint the headband after painting the hair.

BLUE CLOTHING

1. On a retarder-moistened surface, basecoat the jacket, coat and girl's hat with *Ultramarine Blue + Paynes Grey (2:1)*. Dry.

2. On a retarder-moistened surface, shade with *Ultramarine Blue + Paynes Grey (1:1)*. Darken areas with *Paynes Grey*. Dry.

3. Drybrush with *Warm White* to highlight. Using a liner brush, add the folds and light garment edges with *Warm White*. Using same brush, basecoat boy's buttons with *Paynes Grey*; highlight and paint the thread with *Warm White*.

4. Lightly tint shaded areas with *Red Violet*.

YELLOW SCARF AND DRESSES

1. On a retarder-moistened surface, basecoat with *Turners Yellow*. Dry.

2. With your flat brush dressed with *Magic Mix* and sideloaded with *Raw Sienna*, shade folds.

3. Deepen shading with *Burnt Sienna + Paynes Grey (1: touch)*. Using a liner brush, add tassels to scarf ends with *Turners Yellow, Raw Sienna* and *Warm White*.

4. Using *Warm White*, drybrush highlights, then use a liner brush to lighten edges.

5. On a retarder-moistened surface, lightly paint the apron on center girl with *Warm White* to give it the appearance of dotted Swiss organdy. Add tiny dots with *Warm White*. Using a liner brush, dot and border the apron bottom with *Raw Sienna*.

TURQUOISE COAT AND HAT

1. On a retarder-moistened surface, basecoat the hat and coat with *Warm White + Storm Blue (1:1)*. Dry.

2. On a retarder-moistened surface, shade the darker areas with *Storm Blue + Warm White (2:1)*. Dry.

3. Using a flat brush dressed with *Magic Mix* and sideloaded with *Storm Blue*, reinforce the shading in the darker areas and folds. Using a liner brush and *same color*, add buttons and buttonholes.

4. Drybrush *Warm White* to highlight. Using a liner brush, paint the light edges on clothing and buttons with *Warm White*.

COAT TRIM ON TURQUOISE COAT, MITTENS, TEDDY BEAR AND CAT

1. Basecoat the coat trim, yellow mittens, bear and cat with *Naples Yellow Hue + Paynes Grey (1: tiny touch)*. Dry.

2. Flatten the bristles of a round brush between your fingers. On a retarder-moistened surface, use this brush to streak trim, bear and cat with *Raw Sienna + Paynes Grey (1: tiny touch)*. Shade the mittens with the *same color*. Dry.

3. Shade with *Raw Sienna + Burnt Sienna + Paynes Grey (1: touch: touch)*.

4. Using liner brush, paint the edges of the coat trim, cat and bear with the *step 3 color* for a more furry appearance.

5. Using a liner brush, add *Warm White* hairs on the cat's fur, bear and fur collar to lighten the appearance. Use the *same color* to paint the cat's whiskers. Drybrush highlights with *Warm White*. After the face has been painted, use a liner brush to apply *Warm White* dots to highlight the fur collar.

6. Using a liner brush, paint the cat's and bear's eyes, and bear's nose and mouth with *Raw Umber + Paynes Grey (1: touch)*; highlight eyes and nose with a dot of *Warm White*.

7. Tint the shaded areas with *Red Earth*.

WHITE DRESS, SOCKS AND STOCKINGS
1. Shade the original Soft White background with thinned *Paynes Grey*.

2. Using water-thinned *Paynes Grey*, add linework on dress ruffle and stocking cuffs.

BOYS' SCARVES, MITTEN AND SOCK
Scarf on the Right:
1. On a retarder-moistened surface, stipple basecoat with *Nimbus Grey + Raw Umber (1: touch)*. Dry.

2. Stipple right side of scarf with *Nimbus Grey + Raw Umber (1:1)*. Dry. Stipple highlights with *Warm White*.

3. Using a liner brush, add the fringe with *step 1 color*, followed by the *shading color*, and, finally, with *Warm White*.

4. Using a liner brush, paint strokes on the scarf edges with both *step 2 colors*.

5. Shade the folds and darker areas with *Paynes Grey*. Drybrush highlights with *Warm White*.

Scarf on the Left, Mitten and Sock:
1. On a retarder-moistened surface, basecoat with *Nimbus Grey + Raw Umber (1: touch)*. Dry.

2. Using a flat brush, float *Nimbus Grey + Paynes Grey (1:1)* to shade the left side of scarf and the mitten, and to form stripes.

3. Shade the folds and darker areas with *Paynes Grey*. Drybrush a highlight with *Warm White*.

BROWN PANTS AND CENTER GIRL'S BOOTS
1. Basecoat the retarder-moistened surface with *Raw Sienna + Raw Umber + Burnt Sienna (1:1: touch)*. Use a dry brush to soften the paint to create lighter areas. Dry.

2. On a retarder-moistened surface, use the *step 1 color* to darken the folds and deeper areas; add a touch of *Paynes Grey* to the mix if you feel you need more depth of color. Dry. Drybrush *Warm White* to highlight.

3. With your flat brush, float *Warm White* along scalloped edge and the opening of the boot. Using a liner brush, add the boot buttons and lines for holes with *step 1 color + Paynes Grey (1:1)*. Using the same brush, add *Warm White* to highlight the buttons.

GIRLS' SHOES
1. On a retarder-moistened surface, basecoat the shoes with *Paynes Grey*. Dry.

2. Shade the shoes with *Paynes Grey + Raw Umber (1: touch)*.

3. Drybrush *Warm White* to highlight. Using a liner brush, highlight around the opening, on the straps and along soles with *Warm White*.

BLACK BOOTS AND BOY'S SHOE
1. On a retarder-moistened surface, basecoat with *Paynes Grey + Raw Umber (1:1)*. Lighten areas by using your dry brush to soften the color. Dry.

2. Reinforce the darker areas with *step 1 color*.

3. Drybrush highlights with *Warm White*.

4. Using a liner brush, add a lace to the shoe with the *step 1 color*, then highlight with *Warm White*.

TEDDY BEAR'S WAISTCOAT
1. Basecoat with *Nimbus Grey + Warm White (1:1)*.

2. Using a liner brush, paint alternating rows with *Red Earth + Raw Sienna (1:1)* and *Paynes Grey + Warm White (1:1)*.

3. Shade under the head with water-thinned *Paynes Grey*.

4. Highlight the armhole and the lower waistcoat edge with touches of *Warm White*.

FACES AND HANDS
Refer to the color worksheet, using the same colors for the hands. Using a liner brush, basecoat teeth with *Warm White* and float shading with *Ultramarine Blue + Burnt Sienna (2:1)*.

HAIR
Refer to the color worksheet for the left boy and the far-right little girl.

HAIR FOR THE REMAINING THREE CHILDREN
1. Basecoat the hair with *Raw Sienna* and shade with *Raw Sienna + Burnt Sienna (1:1)*.

2. Using a liner brush, paint the strands of hair and girl's curls with *step 1 shading color + Raw Umber (1: touch)*, then with *Warm White*.

WHITE FUR TRIM ON EARMUFFS, AND GIRL'S BONNET AND SLEEVE
1. Stipple these areas with *Warm White* to give them a fluffy appearance. Dry.

2. On a retarder-moistened surface, shade with *Raw Sienna + Paynes Grey (1: touch)*.

3. Using a liner brush, dot the lighter areas *Warm White*.

OWL
1. On a retarder-moistened surface, paint the outer edges of the owl with *Raw Sienna + Raw Umber (1:1)*, softening the color towards the tummy while increasing it above the eyes and beak. Dry.

2. Using a liner brush, paint the body markings with the *step 1 color*.

3. Using the same brush, basecoat the beak and the eyes with *Naples Yellow Hue*, then paint the irises with *step 1 color*. Add pupils with *Paynes Grey*. Highlight the eyes and beak with *Warm White*.

4. Drybrush the body, head and wings with *Warm White*.

5. Tint the left side of the body with a tiny touch of *Red Earth*.

(Continued on Page 10)

Christmas Carolers

(Continued from Page 9)

6. Using a liner brush, paint feet with *step 1 color + Paynes Grey (1: touch)*. Highlight with *Warm White*.

CAROLING BOOKS

1. Basecoat with *Warm White* to tidy the books.

2. Shade with *Paynes Grey* on a retarder-moistened surface. Dry.

3. Using a liner brush, add lettering and design with *Paynes Grey + Raw Umber (1: touch)*.

4. On a retarder-moistened surface, tint with *Yellow Light* to create a glow from the lamplight. *NOTE: If you find Yellow Light is too transparent, add a touch of Warm White.*

   In the same manner, tint the right side of the owl, tops of carolers' heads and bonnets, the right shoulder of the boy on the right and the scarf areas of both boys.

ADDITIONAL SHADING

Evaluate your painting and add more shading and shadows where needed with water-thinned *Paynes Grey*.

WOOD DOOR FRAME AND DOORS

NOTE: Check that the masked areas are still in place. Complete and dry one section at a time.

1. On a retarder-moistened surface, loosely basecoat the wood using a large flat brush and *Raw Sienna + Raw Umber + Paynes Grey (3:1: touch)*. Create the appearance of wood grain by stroking with a fan brush over the wet paint. Dry.

2. Moisten the wood areas with retarder and lightly tint with *Celadon* in some areas. Using an old toothbrush and rubbing alcohol, fleck these areas to give an aged appearance. Dry.

3. Using a liner brush and *step 1 color + Paynes Grey (1: touch)*, paint the knots in the wood and the stress lines.

4. Float the moldings with a flat brush dressed with *Magic Mix* and sideloaded with the *step 3 color*. *NOTE: You may use safe-release masking tape to help keep the lines straight. Ensure your surface is completely dry so you don't pick up wet paint.*

5. Drybrush highlights with *Warm White*.

GARLAND ABOVE DOORWAY AND WREATHS

Refer to the color worksheet for instructions to paint pine boughs, holly and twigs. Leave the masked holly leaves intact until the boughs have been painted. Evaluate your wreath and door top garland and, where needed, shade with *Paynes Grey*.

DOORKNOBS

1. Basecoat with *Naples Yellow Hue*. Dry.

2. Overpaint the knobs with *Pale Gold*.

3. Shade the lower edge of the knobs with *Raw Sienna + Burnt Sienna (1: touch)* and highlight top with a streak of *Warm White*. Shade under the knobs with *Paynes Grey*.

(Continued on Page 13)

Christmas Carolers
Triptych

Center Panel Garland Motif

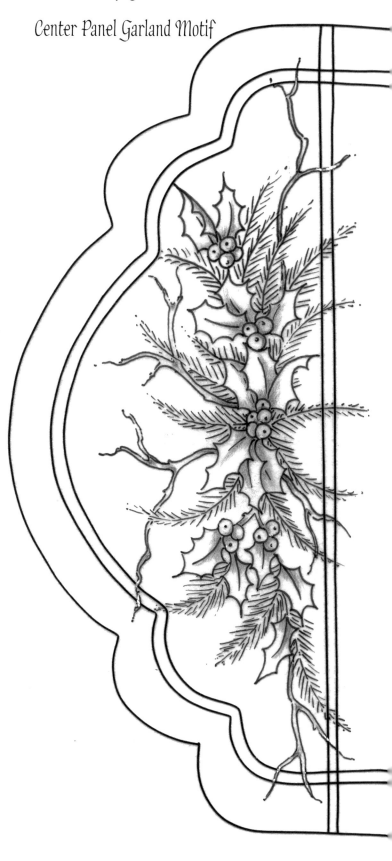

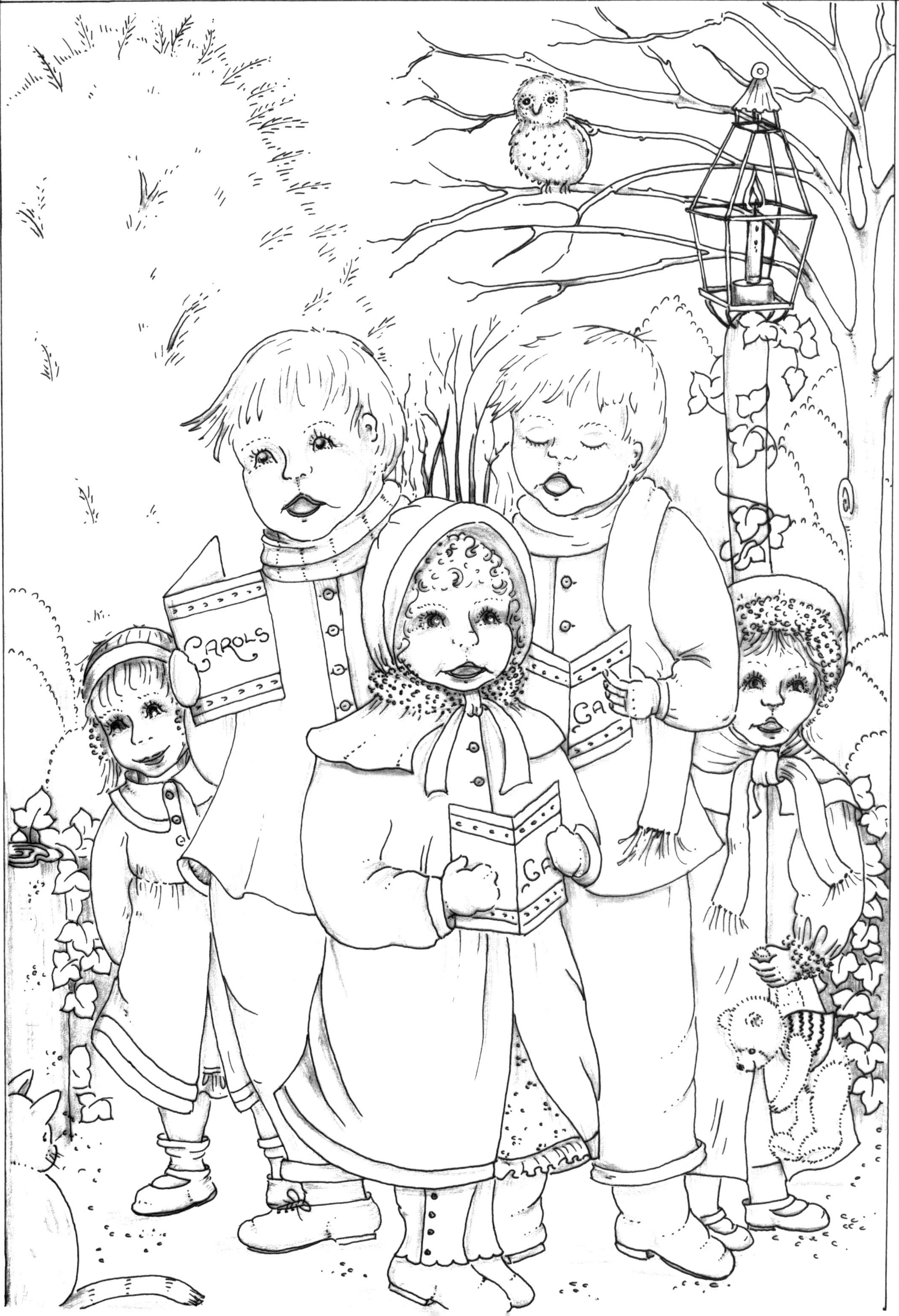
CAROLS

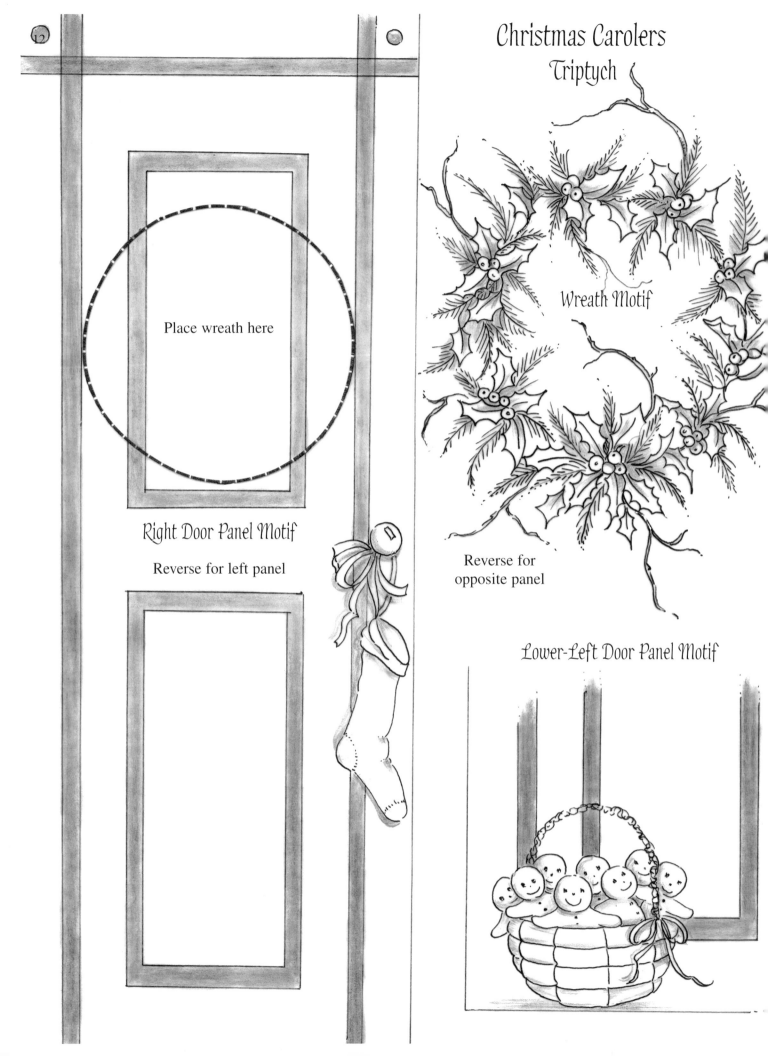

Christmas Carolers
Triptych

Place wreath here

Wreath Motif

Right Door Panel Motif

Reverse for left panel

Reverse for
opposite panel

Lower-Left Door Panel Motif

Christmas Carolers

(Continued from Page 10)

GINGERBREAD MEN

1. Basecoat with *Naples Yellow Hue* and shade with *Raw Sienna*.

2. Shade the deeper areas with *Raw Sienna + Raw Umber + Burnt Sienna (2:1: touch)*.

3. Using a liner brush and *step 2 color*, paint the happy faces and buttons, then dot the eyes with *Warm White*. Drybrush cheeks, heads and arms with *Warm White* to highlight.

BASKET

1. Basecoat with *Nimbus Grey + Raw Umber (1: touch)*.

2. Using a liner brush, paint the basket weave with *Raw Sienna + Raw Umber + Paynes Grey (2:1: touch)*. Using the same brush and *same color mix*, paint "S" strokes on the handle, rim and separation sections. Using the *same mix*, shade the basket.

3. Shade the basket bottom with *Paynes Grey* and dry-brush highlights on the lighter and woven areas with *Warm White*.

4. On a retarder-moistened surface, tint with *Aqua* near the shaded areas and tint with *Yellow Light* in the lighter areas. Tint the left side of handle with *Red Earth*.

CHRISTMAS STOCKING

1. Basecoat with *Nimbus Grey + Warm White (1:1)*. Dry. Overpaint the toe, heel and band areas with *Red Earth*.

2. On a retarder-moistened surface, lightly stipple the light areas of the stocking with *Nimbus Grey + Raw Sienna + Raw Umber (1: touch: touch)*. Stipple more in shaded areas. On the still moist surface, shade the red areas with *Red Earth + Purple Madder (1:1)*.

3. Using a liner brush, paint rows of stitches on the red areas with *red shading color*.

4. Shade inside the stocking opening, below cuff and creases with *Paynes Grey*. Drybrush highlights with *Warm White*.

5. Tint near the shaded areas with *Aqua* on a retarder-moistened surface.

RIBBONS

1. Using a liner brush, basecoat the ribbons with *Naples Yellow Hue*. Dry. Overpaint the ribbons with *Red Earth*.

2. Shade with *Red Earth + Purple Madder (1:1)* and highlight with *Warm White*.

3. Shade behind the basket, gingerbread men, stocking and the ribbons with water-thinned *Paynes Grey*.

(Continued on Page 14)

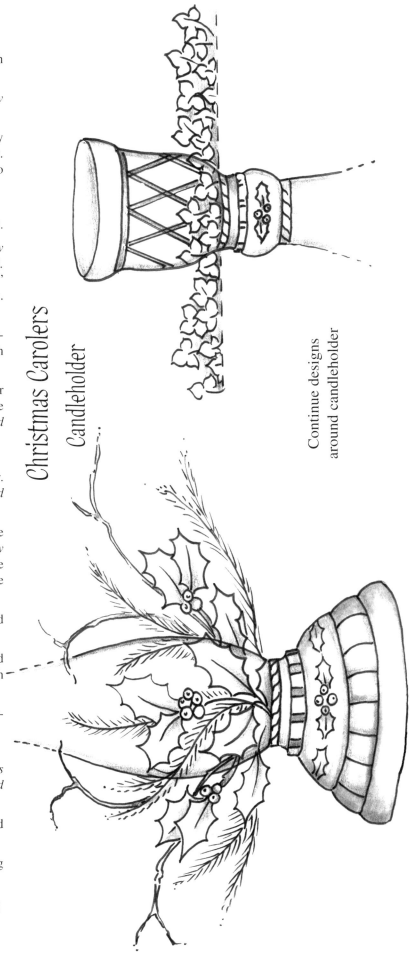

Christmas Carolers
Candleholder

Continue designs around candleholder

Christmas Carolers
(Continued from Page 13)

Candleholder

Starting at the base of the candleholder, paint each band as follows:

1. On a retarder-moistened surface, basecoat with *Raw Sienna + Raw Umber + Paynes Grey (3:1: touch)*. Dry, then overpaint with *Pale Gold*.

2. Basecoat the next two bands with *Ultramarine Blue + Paynes Grey (1:1)*. The stripes on the lower band are floated with *Aqua*. Refer to the color worksheet to paint the holly leaves and berries on upper band.

3. Basecoat the next thin band with *Red Earth*, then paint checks with *Purple Madder*.

4. Paint the next band the same as step 1.

5. Basecoat the next band with *Red Earth*, then paint *Purple Madder* "S" strokes.

6. Refer to "Sky" in the "Triptych" project to paint the larger section of the candleholder and the candle cup; use same colors and technique. Refer to the color worksheet to paint the holly and evergreen boughs on the middle section.

7. Paint the next band the same as step 5 band.

8. Paint the next band the same as step 2 holly band.

9. Paint the next band the same as step 3 band.

10. Paint the next band the same as step 1 band.

11. Paint the next band the same as step 5 band.

12. Using a liner brush, paint the lattice on the candle cup with *Paynes Grey + Raw Umber (1:1)*. Highlight with *Warm White*. Refer to the color worksheet to paint the ivy.

FINISHING
Refer to "Finishing Your Piece" in the General Notes.

Lynchburg Christmas Collection
Color Photo on Front Cover

This collection is dedicated to friends in the Shades of the Blue Ridge Chapter, Virginia.

PALETTE
JO SONJA'S ARTISTS' COLOURS
Aqua
Brilliant Green
Burnt Sienna
Celadon
Gold Oxide
Green Oxide
Jade
Naples Yellow Hue
Nimbus Grey
Paynes Grey
Permanent Alizarine
Purple Madder
Raw Sienna
Raw Umber
Red Earth
Red Oxide
Sapphire
Skin Tone Base
Smoked Pearl
Titanium White
Warm White
Yellow Light
JO SONJA'S BACKGROUND COLOURS
Soft White
JO SONJA'S IRIDESCENT COLOURS
Iridescent Orange

ADDITIONAL MATERIALS
Art masking fluid
Craft wire, 6" of 20-gauge
DecoArt™ Snow-Tex™ Texturizing Medium
Dried moss, as fine as possible
Old toothbrush
Palette knife
Ribbon, 1/4" x 6" for each ornament
Rubbing alcohol, isopropyl
Wire cutters
Wood glue and/or glue gun and glue sticks

BACKGROUND PREPARATION
Please refer to "Basecoating" and "Tracing and Transferring Your Design" at the front of the book.

Basecoat the ornaments with two coats of *Soft White + Clear Glaze Medium (2:1)*.

PAINTING YOUR ORNAMENTS
ARCHWAYS AND BIRD BATH FAUX FINISH
Work each section to completion, dry, and then continue with another section.

1. Paint the archway with retarder-thinned *Smoked Pearl + Raw Sienna + Paynes Grey (1:1: touch)*. Using an old toothbrush, fleck the wet paint with rubbing alcohol. Dry.

2. Moisten the archway with retarder and tint some areas with *Celadon* and other areas with *Burnt Sienna*. Use your fan brush to soften the color. Fleck the tinted areas with rubbing alcohol. Dry.

3. Using *Smoked Pearl + Raw Sienna + Raw Umber + Payne's Grey (4:1:1: touch)*, float the decorative moldings on the archway and base. When dry, transfer your design to the ornament.

4. Refer to the color worksheet for berry and holly leaf colors and instructions. Using a liner brush, paint the twigs around the holly with *Raw Sienna + Raw Umber (1:1)*. Highlight with *Warm White*.

Christmas Tree Ornament

TREE

1. On a retarder-moistened surface, basecoat the tree with *Green Oxide*. Using your fan brush, give the tree a streaked appearance by working from the treetop downwards. Dry.

2. Shade under each branch layer with *Green Oxide + Paynes Grey (2:1)* in the following manner: Using a flat brush dressed with *Magic Mix* and sideloaded with the *shading color*, stand the brush on the chisel edge and use an irregular movement to apply the shading.

3. Using the same method as step 2, lighten the upper side of each tree layer with *Jade + Warm White (1:1)*. Using a liner brush, add highlights near the tree center with *Warm White*. Dry.

4. Drybrush *Warm White* to highlight.

5. On a retarder-moistened surface, tint with *Aqua* in various areas.

6. Basecoat the trunk with *Raw Umber + Raw Sienna + Green Oxide (1:1:1/2)*. Using the *same color mix + Paynes Grey (1: touch)*, shade upper trunk.

BERRIES

Refer to the color worksheet for colors and instructions.

ONE-STROKE HOLLY LEAVES

1. Basecoat the leaves with *Green Oxide*. Float shading with *Green Oxide + Paynes Grey (2:1)*.

2. Using a liner brush, paint the veins and lighten some of the edges with *Warm White*.

(Continued on Page 16)

Lynchburg Christmas Collection

Christmas Tree Ornament

Paint both sides the same

Christmas Tree Ornament

(Continued from Page 15)

3. Shade the tree under the leaves and berries with *Paynes Grey*.

4. On a retarder-moistened surface, tint leaves with a touch of *Aqua* near shaded areas and *Yellow Light* in lighter areas.

RIBBON

1. Using liner brush, basecoat the ribbon with *Naples Yellow Hue*. Shade with *Raw Sienna*, then highlight with *Warm White*.

2. Tint the ribbon with *Iridescent Orange* and shade the tree under the ribbon with thinned *Paynes Grey*.

PLANT POT

1. Basecoat the pot with *Gold Oxide + Raw Sienna (1:1)*.

2. On a retarder-moistened surface, "age" the plant pot with thinned *Green Oxide*.

3. Using the liner brush, paint the cracks in the pot with thinned *Burnt Sienna + Paynes Grey (1:1)*.

Snowman Ornament

SNOWMAN

1. Mask off the cat, scarf and carrot nose with art masking fluid. Dry.

2. Basecoat your snowman with thinned *Smoked Pearl + Nimbus Grey (2:1)*. Dry.

3. On a retarder-moistened surface, shade around the arms, around eyes, under the scarf, under nose and under folds of snow with thinned *Sapphire + Burnt Sienna (1:1)*. On the still slightly moist surface, stipple *Warm White* to create a snowy appearance.

4. On a dry surface, stipple *Titanium White* to highlight the snowman.

5. Remove the masking fluid. Basecoat the nose with thinned *Raw Sienna + Burnt Sienna (1: touch)*. Shade with the *same color*. Highlight with a stroke of *Warm White*.

6. Dot the eyes and mouth with *Paynes Grey + Burnt Sienna (2:1)* and highlight with dots of *Warm White*.

7. On a retarder-moistened surface, tint the shaded areas with *Aqua*.

SCARF

1. Basecoat the various scarf sections with the following colors:
   a. Thinned *Green Oxide*
   b. *Red Oxide + Warm White (1:1)*
   c. Thinned *Raw Sienna*

2. Paint the stitching in each section with the following colors:
   a. Slightly thinned *Green Oxide*. Using a liner brush and the *same color*, add scarf tassels.
   b. *Red Oxide + Warm White (2:1)*
   c. *Raw Sienna + Burnt Sienna (1: touch)*

3. Float shading on the scarf with *Paynes Grey*. If needed, use the *same color* to reinforce shading on snowman around

the scarf, then dot the scarf edges and stitches with *Warm White*.

HAT

1. Basecoat the hat with thinned *Raw Umber + Green Oxide + Raw Sienna (1:1:1)*.

2. First float shading on the hat with *Raw Umber + Green Oxide (2:1)*, then darken shaded areas with a touch of *Paynes Grey*.

3. Using a liner brush, add detail to crown with *Raw Umber + Green Oxide (2:1)*.

4. Using water-thinned *Paynes Grey*, shadow the snowman's head under the hat brim. Highlight hat with *Warm White*.

5. On a retarder-moistened surface, tint some areas of the hat with *Red Earth*.

6. Refer to the color worksheet for colors and instructions to paint holly berries and leaves, including the holly in his hands.

CAT

1. Basecoat with very thin *Raw Sienna* and float shading with *Raw Sienna + Burnt Sienna (1: touch)*.

2. Shade darker areas with the *step 1 shading color + Paynes Grey (1: touch)*.

3. Using a liner brush, paint the nose, eye, inside the ear and whiskers with the *step 2 color*. Give the cat a *Warm White* tummy.

4. Using a liner brush, add dark markings on the fur with *Raw Sienna*.

5. Flatten the bristles of a round brush between your fingers. Using this brush, drybrush highlights on face and ears with *Warm White*.

6. Using water-thinned *Paynes Grey,* shade the snowman next to the cat.

TINTING

On a retarder-moistened surface, tint various areas of the snowman and the green bands on his scarf with thinned *Aqua*.

Santa Ornament

Apply masking fluid to the Teddy bear, Santa's hands, fur trim on clothing and the holly leaves. Dry.

HAT, COAT AND PANTS

1. Basecoat all red areas with *Yellow Light*. Basecoat the coat lining with thinned *Green Oxide + Paynes Grey (2:1)*.

2. On a retarder-moistened surface, overpaint the yellow areas with *Red Earth*. Use more color in the darker areas, less in the lighter areas. Dry.

3. Using *Red Earth + Purple Madder (1:1)*, float shading on the red areas. Darken deep corners with *Paynes Grey*.

4. On a retarder-moistened surface, tint the red clothing with thinned *Permanent Alizarine*. Dry.

(Continued on Page 18)

Snowman
Ornament

Santa
Ornament

Santa Ornament

(Continued from Page 16)

5. Drybrush highlights on the clothing and lining with *Warm White*.

SACK AND BOOTS

1. Basecoat with thinned *Raw Umber + Raw Sienna + Paynes Grey (1:1: touch)*, then shade with the *same color + Paynes Grey (1: touch)*.

2. Using a liner brush, paint the creases in the leather boots and sack with the *shading color*. Drybrush *Warm White* to highlight.

3. On a retarder-moistened surface, tint the boots with *Red Earth* and the lower area of the sack with *Aqua*.

FACE AND HANDS

Remove the masking fluid.

1. Basecoat the face and hands with *Skin Tone Base*.

2. On a retarder-moistened face, shade around the hairline, eye sockets, and side and base of the nose with *Burnt Sienna*. Soften this color with your dry brush. On the still moist surface, tint the cheeks with very thin *Red Earth + Permanent Alizarine (1: touch)* and soften the color.

3. Paint the irises with *Sapphire*, then paint pupils with *Paynes Grey*. Add a touch of *Warm White* to the corner of each eye and a *Warm White* sparkle to the pupils. Using a liner brush and thinned *Burnt Sienna*, outline the eyes and paint the age lines.

4. On a dry surface, drybrush *Warm White* on the cheeks and the tip of the nose.

5. Using a liner brush, add eyebrows and lashes with *Smoked Pearl + Nimbus Grey (2:1)*. Shade the hairs with strokes of thinned *Sapphire + Burnt Sienna (1:1)*. Highlight with *Warm White*.

6. Shade the hands with thinned *Burnt Sienna*.

7. Using a liner brush, paint the nails with thinned *Burnt Sienna + Paynes Grey (1: touch)*. Highlight the nails and hands with *Warm White*.

HAIR, BEARD AND MOUSTACHE

1. Basecoat the hair and beard with *Smoked Pearl + Nimbus Grey (2:1)*. Shade with *Sapphire + Burnt Sienna (1:1)*.

2. Using a liner brush, add hairs first with the *shade color*, then with *Warm White*.

3. Using a liner brush, paint the moustache with *step 1 basecoat color*, then paint hairs with *shade color* and *Warm White*.

4. On a retarder-moistened surface, tint the shaded areas with very thin *Aqua*.

TEDDY BEAR

1. Basecoat with *Raw Sienna*, then shade with *Raw Sienna + Raw Umber + Burnt Sienna (2:1: tiny touch)*.

2. Dot the eyes and nose with *Raw Umber + Paynes Grey (1:1)* and highlight with *Warm White* dots.

3. On a retarder-moistened surface, tint darker areas with *Red Earth*. Tint *Aqua* near shaded areas.

4. Drybrush *Warm White* to highlight.

FUR TRIM

1. Loosely basecoat the trim with thin *Raw Sienna*.

2. On a retarder-moistened surface, stipple *Warm White*. Dry.

3. Shade the trim with thinned *Paynes Grey*, then stipple *Titanium White* to highlight.

4. Moisten the trim with retarder and tint near the shaded areas with *Aqua*.

BELT AND BUCKLE

1. Basecoat the belt with *Raw Umber + Paynes Grey (1:1)*. Highlight with *Warm White*.

2. Using a liner brush, basecoat buckle with *Naples Yellow Hue*, then overpaint with thinned *Raw Sienna*. Using a liner brush, add *Warm White* highlights.

BERRIES

Refer to color worksheet for colors and instructions.

ONE-STROKE HOLLY LEAVES

1. Basecoat the leaves with *Green Oxide*. Float shading with *Green Oxide + Paynes Grey (2:1)*.

2. Using a liner brush, paint the veins and lighten some of the edges with *Warm White*.

3. On a retarder-moistened surface, tint with a touch of *Aqua* near shaded areas and *Yellow Light* in lighter areas.

4. Basecoat the twigs with *Raw Sienna + Raw Umber (1:1)*. Highlight with *Warm White*.

Cardinals Ornament

Basecoat the male and female cardinals with *Naples Yellow Hue*.

FEMALE CARDINAL

I love to see this shy little bird; the color combination of her plumage is exquisite. I hope you enjoy painting her as much as I have.

1. On a retarder-moistened surface, paint the breast and neck areas with *Naples Yellow Hue + Gold Oxide (1:1)*. On the still moist surface, paint *Red Earth + Paynes Grey (1: touch)* on her crest, breast, lower wing and tail feathers. Using the *same color*, tint the beak very thinly.

2. Using a liner brush and *Raw Umber + Paynes Grey (1:1)*, paint the center of the eye and the dark feathers around the beak. Dry.

3. Moisten the cardinal with retarder. Using *Raw Umber + Warm White (1:1)*, paint the grey feathers on the back and wing. Add touches of this color to the area below the crest, below the wing feathers and the forehead area.

4. Using a liner brush and *step 3 color*, add a few lines to suggest overlapping feathers.

5. Using the *step 3 color + touch of Paynes Grey*, float shading around the outer edges of the grey areas.

6. Using a liner brush, highlight the upper sides of the upper flight feathers with *Warm White*. Add touches of this color to the lower area of her tummy.

7. Using the same brush, add a thin band around her eyes with *Naples Yellow Hue + Warm White (1:1)*. Using the liner brush and thinned *step 3 color*, outline the yellow eye band. Add a *Warm White* dot to highlight eyes.

8. Using a liner brush, paint the beak separation and nostril with *Raw Umber + Paynes Grey (1:1)*. Highlight the beak with *Warm White*.

9. Moisten the entire cardinal with retarder and tint the red areas and the beak with *Permanent Alizarine*. Dry.

10. Highlight the feathers with touches of *Warm White*.

MALE CARDINAL

This little fellow is far less complicated because of the all over red color.

1. On a retarder-moistened surface, basecoat the cardinal with *Red Earth*, then give shape to his body by softening the color with your dry brush. Dry.

2. Paint the beak with very thin *Red Earth*.

3. Using a liner brush, paint the dark feathers around the beak with *Raw Umber + Paynes Grey (1:1)*.

4. Using a liner brush, suggest wing feathers with *Red Earth + Paynes Grey (1:1)*.

5. Refer to female cardinal for the eye and beak.

6. On a retarder-moistened surface, tint the red feathering with thinned *Permanent Alizarine*. Dry.

7. Highlight with touches of *Warm White*.

FINISHING

Refer to "Finishing Your Piece" in the General Notes.

For each ornament, cut and fold over a 6" length of ribbon. Moisten the ends with glue, roll and pinch together. Dry. Add glue to the joined ends and secure in the top of the archway.

Referring to the photo, glue items into position in the arches; the tree trunk goes through the pot into the base of the arch.

For the cardinal ornament, cut two short lengths of 20-gauge wire. Glue into bottom of female cardinal, then into the base of the arch.

Using your glue gun, attach the moss in and around the ornament bases, in the tree pot, and on some post caps.

Using your palette knife and *textural medium*, add touches of snow on moss, birdbath, on each base and on post caps.

Lynchburg Christmas Collection

Cardinals Ornament

Cardinals are painted
the same on both sides

Christmas Bowl

Color Photo on Page 23

PALETTE

JO SONJA'S ARTISTS' COLOURS

Amethyst	Permanent Alizarine
Antique Green	Purple Madder
Aqua	Raw Umber
Brilliant Green	Red Earth
Burgundy	Storm Blue
Green Light	Teal Green
Green Oxide	Warm White
Naples Yellow Hue	Yellow Light
Paynes Grey	

JO SONJA'S BACKGROUND COLOURS

Claret Rose

JO SONJA'S METALLIC COLOURS

Rich Gold

ADDITIONAL MATERIALS

Art masking fluid
Old toothbrush
Rubbing alcohol, isopropyl
Wooden bowl, 9"

BACKGROUND PREPARATION

Please refer to "Basecoating" and "Tracing and Transferring Your Design" at the front of the book.

Basecoat the entire bowl with two coats of *Claret Rose + Clear Glaze Medium (2:1)*. When dry, transfer only the basic design to your bowl. You will find it much easier to freehand the evergreen boughs.

PAINTING YOUR DESIGN

Basecoat the following with two coats of paint:
Plums: *Naples Yellow Hue*
Plum Leaves: *Green Oxide*
Holly Leaves: *Antique Green*
Holly Berries: *Naples Yellow Hue*

PLUMS

1. On a retarder-moistened surface, paint the entire plum with *Burgundy*. Using a dry round brush, stipple the plum surface, softening the color in lighter areas. Complete all plums and dry.

2. On a retarder-moistened surface, shade with *Purple Madder*. In lighter areas, add a touch of *Burgundy* to the color. On the still moist surface, paint *Amethyst* in the lightest areas. Stipple these colors to soften. Complete all the plums and dry. Drybrush highlights with *Warm White*.

PLUM LEAVES

1. On a retarder-moistened surface, shade the leaves with *Green Oxide + Paynes Grey (2:1)*. You may need to vary this mix by adding a touch more *Paynes Grey* for darker areas. On the same moist surface, highlight with *Yellow Light*. Paint all plum leaves to this stage and dry.

2. Using a liner brush, paint the veins and light leaf edges with *Warm White + Green Oxide (1: touch)*.

3. Using a liner brush, add bug bites on or near the edges of some leaves with *Purple Madder;* highlight part of the bug bite opening with *Warm White*.

4. On a retarder-moistened surface, tint the leaves with *Green Light* in lighter areas and add touches of *Aqua* near the shaded areas. Soften these tints with a dry brush.

5. Drybrush *Warm White* to highlight leaves.

HOLLY LEAVES

1. Referring to the plum leaves steps 1 and 2, paint the holly leaves.

2. Tint the lighter leaf areas with *Brilliant Green* and near the shaded areas with *Aqua*. Dry.

3. Drybrush *Warm White* to highlight.

HOLLY BERRIES

1. Dress a flat brush with *Magic Mix* and touch brush corner into *Red Earth*. Paint a "C" stroke to form one side of each berry; dry. Paint the opposite side of each berry with another "C" stroke to complete the round berry.

2. With your flat brush dressed with *Magic Mix* and a touch of *Purple Madder* on the corner of your brush, float shading on the berries.

3. Using a liner brush, paint each seed with a dot of *Purple Madder + Paynes Grey (1:1)*.

4. Highlight the lighter berries with a dot of *Warm White* and lightly tint the berries with *Permanent Alizarine*.

NOTE: Dry all painting thoroughly before proceeding to the evergreen boughs.

EVERGREEN BOUGHS

1. Mask off the painted areas with masking fluid. This will give you more freedom to freehand the evergreen boughs.

2. Load an old, fluffed-out 1/4" angular brush with *Teal Green*, then pick up *Green Oxide* on the tip. Stipple the foliage working from the tip of the bough.

3. In the same manner, stipple with *Storm Blue + Warm White (1:1)* to lighten. Complete the evergreen boughs as shown and dry thoroughly.

4. Using a liner brush and *Warm White*, dot the lighter areas of the boughs.

5. Remove masking. Using your angle brush and *evergreen colors*, add touches of foliage to the edges of some plums and leaves. Add a small touch of *Paynes Grey* to the center of each bough.

TWIGS

1. Using a liner brush, basecoat the twigs with *Raw Umber + Warm White (1: touch)*.

(Continued on Page 22)

21

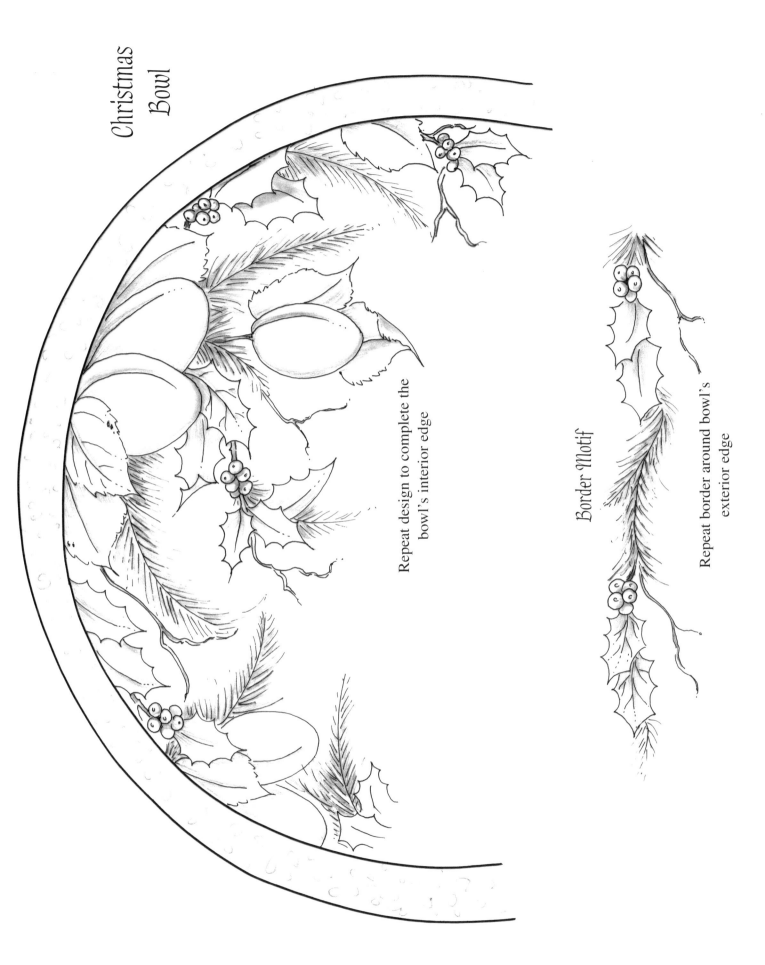

Christmas Bowl

Repeat design to complete the bowl's interior edge

Border Motif

Repeat border around bowl's exterior edge

Christmas Bowl

(Continued from Page 20)

2. Shade with *Raw Umber + Paynes Grey (1: touch)*, then highlight with touches of *Warm White*.

ADDITIONAL SHADING

To give more dimension to your painting, float shading to the right and below plums, leaves and berries on the inside of the bowl with *Paynes Grey + Purple Madder (1:1)*. Float shading below the leaves and berries on the outside of the bowl with the same color.

BOWL EDGE

On a retarder-moistened surface, paint the edge with *Rich Gold*. Using an old toothbrush and rubbing alcohol, fleck the gold to give you a hammered gold appearance. Dry.

FINISHING

Refer to "Finishing Your Piece" in the General Notes.

Captain PJ's Curiosity Shop and Santa's Folly

Color Photos on Pages 26 and 27

PALETTE

JO SONJA'S ARTISTS' COLOURS

Aqua	Raw Umber
Burnt Sienna	Red Earth
Green Oxide	Red Violet (Santa)
Jade	Skin Tone Base (Santa)
Naples Yellow Hue	Smoked Pearl
Nimbus Grey	Storm Blue
Pacific Blue (Santa)	Teal Green (Santa)
Paynes Grey	Titanium White
Purple Madder	Warm White
Raw Sienna	Yellow Deep

JO SONJA'S BACKGROUND COLOURS

Soft White

ADDITIONAL MATERIALS

Art masking fluid
Pearl thread, 1 yard
Wood glue

BACKGROUND PREPARATION

Please refer to "Basecoating" and "Tracing and Transferring Your Design" at the front of the book.

Basecoat the ornament pieces with two coats of *Soft White + Clear Glaze Medium (2:1)*. Dry.

Before transferring the pattern, cut the traced design to fit the ornament shape. Secure it with masking tape. Gently transfer only the basic design lines.

Apply art masking fluid for protection to the following areas:

Curiosity Shop: Door and window frames, signboards, seagulls, buoys, lighthouse lamp, Christmas tree, boat at back of shop, posts, bell and all items in the shop window.

Santa's Folly: Fish, edge of Christmas tree, Santa and seagull.

PAINTING YOUR ORNAMENTS

Captain PJ's Curiosity Shop

WALLS

1. Using a flat brush dressed with *Magic Mix* and sideloaded with *Red Earth + Raw Umber (2:1)*, start under the roof and float each section of the siding.

2. Shade under the roof by adding a touch of *Payne's Grey* to the *step 1 color*. Randomly add some *Aqua* tints on walls.

ROOF SHINGLES

1. On a retarder-moistened surface, basecoat the roof with *Warm White + Raw Umber + Paynes Grey (2:1:1)*. Use a fan brush to even the brush strokes. Dry.

2. Dress a flat brush with *Magic Mix* and sideload with *Raw Umber + Warm White + Paynes Grey (2:1:1)*. Start at the top of the roof and float shading to separate the layers of shingles.

3. Float *Warm White* to lighten some of the overlapping shingles.

4. Using your liner brush and *step 2 color + Paynes Grey (1: touch)*, paint cracks on the shingles to add separation and aging.

5. On a retarder-moistened surface, tint the roof with *Paynes Grey, Raw Sienna* and *Aqua*. Be careful not to mix these colors.

WINDOWPANES

Paint each window separately. On a retarder-moistened surface, basecoat the window with *Raw Umber + Paynes Grey (1:1)*, then even the brush strokes with a fan brush. Dry. The inner window frames will be painted later. Remove masking.

CHIMNEY, PATHWAY AND STEPS

1. On a retarder-moistened surface, basecoat with *Smoked Pearl + Raw Sienna + Paynes Grey (3:1: touch)*. Dry.

2. Use a flat brush dressed with *Magic Mix* and sideloaded with *Smoked Pearl + Raw Sienna + Raw Umber + Paynes Grey (2:2:1: touch)* to float shading to form the chimney stones and doorsteps. Use the *same color* to shade chimney, pathway and steps.

3. Drybrush *Warm White* to highlight the stones and the upper area of the steps.

4. On a retarder-moistened surface, stipple some areas of the pathway with *Raw Sienna* and other areas with *Green Oxide* to give it a moss-like appearance.

5. If needed, intensify the shading around the base of the steps and the posts with *Paynes Grey*.

(Continued on Page 24)

Christmas Carolers

Pages 7-14

Christmas Bowl

Pages 20-22

Captain PJ's Curiosity Shop
(Continued from Page 22)

POSTS

Basecoat, shade, highlight, detail and tint with the *roof shingle colors.*

DOOR AND WINDOW FRAMES, DOORS AND SIGNBOARDS

NOTE: Paint the objects in the shop window prior to painting the inner window framework.

1. On a retarder-moistened surface, basecoat all wood areas with *Smoked Pearl + Raw Sienna + Paynes Grey (3:1: touch).* Dry.

2. Using *Smoked Pearl + Raw Sienna + Raw Umber + Paynes Grey (2:2:1: touch),* float shading on the wood areas.

3. Highlight with *Warm White.*

4. On a retarder-moistened surface, tint some areas of the wood with touches of *Raw Sienna* and other areas with *Aqua.*

5. Using a liner brush, paint two stake legs below lower sign with *Paynes Grey.* Highlight with *Warm White.*

6. When you are ready to paint the inner window framework, use a liner brush to basecoat the framework on all windows with *Warm White.* Complete these inner frames following the colors given for the window frames. Shade and highlight with a liner brush.

7. After painting the objects in the shop window, float shading on the window next to the window frame with *Paynes Grey.* Drybrush highlights on door and windowpanes, except shop window, with *Warm White.*

8. On the back of the shop, tint windowpanes near shaded areas with *Aqua.*

ROWBOATS AND SAILBOATS (in the window and on sign)

1. Using a flat brush dressed with *Magic Mix* and sideloaded with *Storm Blue + Raw Umber (1: touch),* float shading on the Soft White rowboats along the top, inside the boat on the back and under each overlapping board. Using the *same color,* paint the outside of the sailboat hulls.

2. Float *Warm White* to lighten the edge of the boards on rowboats and to highlight the sailboats.

3. Basecoat the inside of the sailboats with *Raw Sienna + Raw Umber (1: touch).*

4. Shade the sails and the hulls of all boats with *Paynes Grey.*

5. Using a liner brush, basecoat the sailboat masts with *Paynes Grey + Raw Umber (1:1).* Highlight the masts and edges of the hulls with *Warm White.*

6. Drybrush some areas of the rowboats with *Raw Umber* and other areas with *Red Earth + Raw Umber (1: touch)* to age them.

7. Using a liner brush, add lettering to rowboat on the back with *Storm Blue + Raw Umber (1: touch).*

SEAGULLS

1. On the Soft White background, basecoat the wings and tail feathers with *Nimbus Grey + Warm White (1:1).*

2. Paint the tips of the wings and tail with *Paynes Grey + Raw Umber (1:1).*

3. On a retarder-moistened surface, shade the outer edges of the head and breast, around the beak and the eye depression with *step 1 color.* Dry.

4. Basecoat the beak with *Naples Yellow Hue + Raw Sienna (1: touch).* Shade the beak with thinned *Burnt Sienna.* Paint the eye, beak separation and nostril with *step 2 color.* When dry, add a tiny dot of *Warm White* to the eye to add a sparkle. Using a liner brush and *step 1 color,* line around the eyes.

5. Using a liner brush, paint legs and feet with *Naples Yellow Hue.* In most cases they are tiny lines that are shaded with a line of the *step 2 color* and highlighted with *Warm White.*

6. Drybrush *Titanium White* highlights on head, wing and breast.

DECOYS

CURLEWS ("tall" bird)

1. Tint the Soft White birds with *Raw Sienna + Raw Umber (1: touch).* Using the *same color* and a liner brush, paint the wooden legs, beaks and the body markings.

2. Using a liner brush, paint the eyes and a line under beaks with thinned *Paynes Grey + Raw Umber (1:1).* Using the same brush, add highlights to the eyes, bodies and legs with *Warm White.*

DUCK

1. Basecoat the duck's head and back with *Storm Blue + Raw Umber (1: touch);* vary the color. Drybrush highlights with *Warm White.* Paint the breast area with *Raw Sienna + Raw Umber (1: touch).* Paint the wing and tail feathers with *Nimbus Grey + White (1:1).*

2. Basecoat the beak with *Naples Yellow Hue + Raw Sienna (1: touch).* Tint with very thin *Burnt Sienna.* Highlight with *Warm White.*

3. Paint the eye the same as the curlews.

GLASS FLOAT IN THE NET

1. Tint the Soft White float with thinned *Storm Blue + Raw Umber (1: touch).*

2. Using a liner brush, paint the net with *Paynes Grey + Raw Umber (1:1).* Using same brush and *Warm White,* add highlights to the net and dots to the float.

BASKET

1. Basecoat with *Naples Yellow Hue*.

2. Using your flat brush dressed with *Magic Mix* and side-loaded with *Raw Sienna*, float shading on the basket to create its shape. Using a liner brush and *same color*, paint the handle.

3. Deepen the shading with *Raw Sienna + Raw Umber (1:1)*. Paint the weave on the basket using a liner brush and the *same color*.

4. With same brush, paint the basket and handle edges with *Warm White*.

5. Tint the basket with very thin *Burnt Sienna*.

LIGHTHOUSE

1. On the Soft White background, paint the three bands and the door with *Red Earth*. Paint the light on the top with *Yellow Deep*. Paint the windows with *Paynes Grey + Raw Umber (1: touch)*.

2. Float shading on left side of lighthouse with thinned *Paynes Grey*.

3. Stipple thinned *Green Oxide* next to base of the lighthouse.

4. Using a liner brush, add the casing around the dome with *Paynes Grey + Raw Umber (1:1)*. Using the same brush, highlight the casings with *Warm White*.

5. Drybrush *Warm White* down the center of the building to create the impression of a rounded building.

CHRISTMAS TREES

1. On a retarder-moistened surface and using your round brush, loosely basecoat the trees with *Green Oxide*. Dry.

2. Using *Green Oxide + Paynes Grey (2:1)*, float shading under branches.

3. Using *Jade + Warm White (1:1)*, float highlights on the top side of the branches. As you get closer to the center of the tree, add more *Warm White* to the color.

4. Using a liner brush, add individual needles with the *step 2 color* and in the lighter areas with the *step 3 color*.

5. Drybrush *Warm White* highlights.

FOLIAGE ABOVE THE SIGNBOARD, WINDOWS AND ON DOORS

1. Paint clusters of tiny one-stroke leaves with *Green Oxide*.

(Continued on Page 28)

Captain PJ's Curiosity Shop

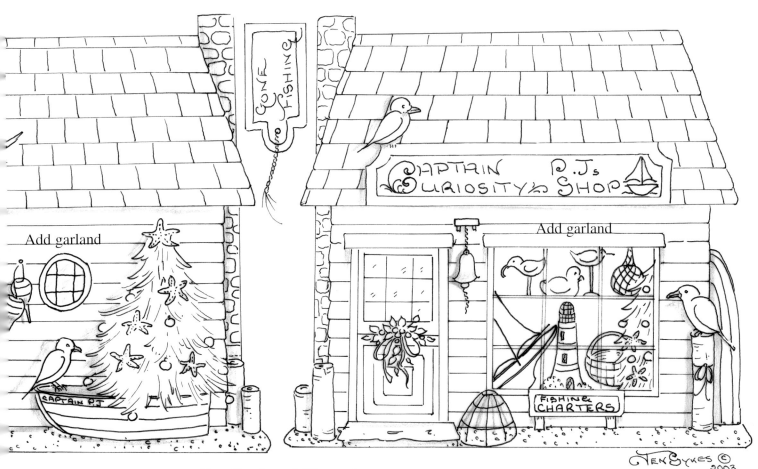

Tag: Cut from 1/8" wood
Ornament: Cut from 1/4" wood
Drill holes for thread

Captain PJ's
Curiosity Shop and
Santa's Folly
Pages 22, 24-25, 28-29 & 31

Schoolhouse

Pages 44-48 & 50-51

Bears and Berries

Pages 36-39

Captain PJ's Curiosity Shop

Pages 22, 24-25, 28-29 & 31

Village Toy Shop

Pages 44-48 & 50-51

Captain PJ'S Curiosity Shop
(Continued from Page 25)

2. Shade with *Green Oxide + Paynes Grey (2:1)* and high-light with *Warm White*.

BERRIES AND CHRISTMAS TREE BAUBBLES
Refer to the color worksheet to complete.

RIBBONS
1. Using a liner brush, basecoat ribbons with *Red Earth*, then highlight with *Warm White*.

2. Shade beneath the left side of the ribbons with water-thinned *Paynes Grey*.

STARFISH
1. Basecoat with *Naples Yellow Hue*, then tint with very thin *Burnt Sienna*. Highlight with tiny dots of *Warm White*.

2. Shade under the lower edge of each starfish's tendrils with thinned *Paynes Grey*.

CANDLEHOLDER, BELL AND DOORKNOBS
1. Basecoat with *Raw Umber + Warm White + Paynes Grey (2:1:1)*. Shade with *Paynes Grey + Raw Umber (1:1)* and highlight with *Warm White*.

2. Basecoat candle with *Naples Yellow Hue + Warm White (1:1)*, then tint with *Aqua*. Highlight with *Warm White*.

3. Using a liner brush, add the wick with *Paynes Grey + Raw Umber (1:1)*.

LETTERING ON SIGNBOARDS
1. Using thinned *Storm Blue + Raw Umber (1: touch)* and a liner brush, paint the lettering and embellishments.

2. Highlight the lettering and embellishments on the large sign with touches of *Warm White*.

BUOYS HANGING BY THE BACK DOOR
1. On the Soft White background, paint *Red Earth* stripes on one of the buoys and *Storm Blue* stripes on the other. Shade the buoys with *Paynes Grey*.

2. Highlight each one with a *Warm White* line down the center.

ROPES HOLDING BUOYS AND BELL, AND ON CHRISTMAS TREE
1. Using a liner brush, paint the ropes with *Smoked Pearl + Raw Sienna (1: touch)*.

2. Using the same brush, paint "S" strokes along the ropes with *Raw Sienna + Paynes Grey (1: touch)*, then highlight with touches of *Warm White*.

LOBSTER POT
1. Using liner brush, basecoat the pot with *Smoked Pearl + Raw Sienna (1: touch)*. Overpaint with *Raw Sienna + Paynes Grey (1: touch)*.

2. Shade with thinned *Paynes Grey*, then highlight with touches of *Warm White*.

SHADOWS
Using your round brush and water-thinned *Paynes Grey*, paint the shadows on walls and roof next to gulls, posts, bell, tree and buoys.

TINTING YOUR ORNAMENT
Although I have given tinting colors for various items throughout this book, I always review my painting and add additional tints. Always tint on a retarder- or water-moistened surface. Tint the Christmas trees, boats, breasts of seagulls, foliage, under the eaves of the shingles, and the base of the walls with *Aqua*. *Paynes Grey* is a lovely shading tint where you feel you need more depth of color.

GONE FISHING TAG
Refer to the instructions for the signboards, including the lettering.

Santa's Folly

BACKGROUND
1. On a retarder-moistened surface, paint the entire sky area with *Teal Green + Paynes Grey (1:1)*. Use a fan brush to even the strokes. Dry.

2. Moisten this area with retarder and darken the area at the top with *Paynes Grey* and lighten the lower area with *Aqua*. Soften your brush strokes to give a blended appearance. Dry.

3. Moisten the top area with retarder, then tint the darkness with *Red Violet* to give the color more warmth.

BOAT
1. On a retarder-moistened surface, basecoat the entire boat with *Nimbus Grey + Warm White (2:1)*. Dry.

2. Using a flat brush dressed with *Magic Mix* and sideloaded with *Nimbus Grey*, float shading under each overlapping board.

3. Float *Warm White* to lighten the edges of the boards. Dry.

4. On a retarder-moistened surface, shade the front and rear of the boat with thinned *Storm Blue + Raw Umber (1: touch)*. Dry.

5. To give the boat an interesting aged appearance, drybrush some areas with *Raw Sienna* and other areas with *Red Earth*.

6. Using liner brush, paint the boat's name using *step 4 color*. Use the *same color* to add some grain lines to the boards.

SANTA
1. Basecoat the coat with *Naples Yellow Hue*, the pants with *Raw Sienna + Paynes Grey (1: touch)*, and the face and hands with *Skin Tone Base*.

2. On a retarder-moistened surface, overpaint the coat with *Red Earth* and shade the trousers with *Raw Umber + Green Oxide (2:1)*. Using a liner brush, basecoat the belt with *Raw Umber + Paynes Grey (1:1)*. Dry. Using a liner brush, paint

the belt buckle with *Naples Yellow Hue;* tint with thin *Burnt Sienna.*

3. Using *Purple Madder,* float shading the darker areas of the coat. Drybrush *Warm White* highlights on coat, pants and belt.

4. Stipple the sleeve cuff with *Warm White* and shade with *Raw Sienna.*

5. On a retarder-moistened surface, shade the face and hands with thinned *Burnt Sienna.* Blush the cheeks and tip of his nose with thinned *Red Earth + Warm White (1: touch).* Paint the eyes with a dot of *Pacific Blue.* When dry, shade the dots with *Paynes Grey.* Using *Warm White,* paint the corner beside each eyeball and a dot to give the eyes sparkle. Using *Purple Madder,* float a tiny "C" stroke to form the open mouth. Highlight the cheeks and the tip of his nose with *Warm White.* Dry.

6. On a retarder-moistened surface, basecoat the hair and beard with *Nimbus Grey + Warm White + Raw Sienna (2:1: touch).* Dry. Using the *same color* and a liner brush, paint individual hair strands; add a touch of *Paynes Grey* to this color, if needed. Using the same brush, add *Warm White* hair strands.

7. Using the *hair colors,* paint eyelashes, eyebrows and moustache. Drybrush *Titanium White* to highlight the hair and the beard.

FISH TAG AND HAND-HELD FISH

1. Basecoat the fish with *Nimbus Grey + Warm White (1:1).* Shade with *Nimbus Grey* and highlight with *Warm White.*

2. Dot the eyes with *Naples Yellow Hue + Raw Sienna (1: touch).* Using *Paynes Grey + Raw Umber (1: touch),* paint the pupils and inside of mouth. Thin this color, then use a liner brush to outline each eye and the gill areas.

3. Using liner brush, add thinned *Paynes Grey* scales to side of fish. Using *Warm White,* dot pupils, paint mouth opening and add highlight lines next to the gills and scales.

RAINBOW TROUT

1. On a retarder-moistened surface, softly blend the following thinned colors, then dry:
   Tail and Fins: *Raw Sienna + Raw Umber (1: touch)*
   Upper Body Area: *Aqua*
   Mid Body Area: *Red Earth*
   Tummy Area: *Warm White*

2. Using a liner brush, paint eyes and scales following instructions for the hand-held fish.

FISHING POLE AND LINE

1. Using a liner brush, basecoat the pole with *Warm White.* Overpaint the pole with *Raw Umber + Green Oxide (2:1).*

2. Using a liner brush, paint the line guides on the pole with *Paynes Grey + Raw Umber (1:1).* Highlight the pole and line guides with touches of *Warm White.*

3. Using a liner brush, paint the fishing line with *Nimbus Grey + Warm White (1:1).*

BUBBLES

1. Using your flat brush dressed with *Magic Mix* and side-loaded with *Warm White,* float one side of each bubble with a tiny "C" stroke, varying the size of each bubble.

2. Using the *same color* and a liner brush, paint the opposite side of the "C" stroke to complete the shape of the bubble.

REMAINING DETAILS

Using your flat brush, float *Paynes Grey* shadows on background next to the pole, fish and seagulls.

Refer to "Captain PJ'S Curiosity Shop" for instructions on the following: Christmas tree, starfish, lobster pots, the foliage

(Continued on Page 31)

Santa's Folly

Fish: Cut from 1/8" wood
Ornament: Cut from 1/4" wood
Drill holes for thread

Clowns for Christmas

Pages 31-35

Santa's Folly

(Continued from Page 29)

on Santa's headband and the seagulls. Refer to the "Village Toy Shop" to paint the berries.

TINTING

Moisten the entire ornament with retarder and tint with *Aqua* on Santa's hair, beard, breasts of the seagulls, sleeve cuff fur, Christmas tree, lobster pots, seagulls, and the grey fish.

Buoy and Book Ornaments

1. Paint stripes on one buoy with *Red Earth* and on the other with *French Blue + Warm White (1:1)*. Tint the buoys with touches of *Raw Sienna + Raw Umber (1: touch)*. Tint some areas with *Aqua*.

2. Basecoat the anchor on the book with *Nimbus Grey + Warm White (1:1)*. Shade anchor with thinned *Storm Blue + Raw Umber (1: touch)*. Highlight with *Warm White*. Paint the lettering with thinned *Storm Blue + Raw Umber (1: touch)*. Highlight letters with *Warm White*.

3. Refer to "Captain PJ's Curiosity Shop" to paint the foliage, rope and seagulls. Refer to "Village Toy Shop" to paint berries. Refer to "Santa's Folly" to paint hand-held fish and fishing pole.

FINISHING

Refer to "Finishing Your Piece" in the General Instructions.

CURIOSITY SHOP AND SANTA: Glue a 2" strand of thread to the fish and sign. Cut three 6" strands of thread and braid. When you have braided three-fourths of the length, add the thread for the small wooden item and continue braiding until complete. Fold over and glue the two ends. Roll ends between your fingertips to roll the threads together. Dry. Add glue into top hole and place braided thread into hole. Dry.

BUOYS AND SHIP'S LOG: Glue one end of thread into hole in top of buoy. Wrap thread around top of buoy, then coil the remaining thread and glue on flat area. Glue another strand of thread into the hole in top of buoy, then join to book. Glue a small piece of thread to the bottom hole of the book. Glue seagull to buoy.

Ship's Log   Buoy

Buoy and Book Ornaments

Clowns for Christmas

Color Photo on Page 30

PALETTE
JO SONJA'S ARTISTS' COLOURS
Aqua
Burgundy
Burnt Sienna
Paynes Grey
Permanent Alizarine
Purple Madder
Raw Umber
Titanium White
Ultramarine Blue
Warm White
Yellow Oxide
JO SONJA'S BACKGROUND COLOURS
Soft White
JO SONJA'S IRIDESCENT COLOURS
Blue Iridescent
Red Iridescent
JO SONJA'S METALLIC COLOURS
Pale Gold

ADDITIONAL MATERIALS
Art masking fluid
Craft wire, 6 1/2"
Needle, large-eyed
Ribbon or floss, 8" burgundy for each hanging loop
Ribbon, 1/4" x 6" burgundy
Wood glue or glue gun and glue sticks
Wooden balls, 1/2" diameter with 3/32" hole

BACKGROUND PREPARATION
Please refer to "Basecoating" and "Tracing and Transferring Your Design" at the front of the book.

(Continued on Page 32)

32

Clowns for Christmas

(Continued from Page 31)

Basecoat the clowns and balls with two coats of *Soft White + Clear Glaze Medium (2:1)*. When dry, transfer basic design lines to the clowns.

Mask ruffled collars and socks.

PAINTING YOUR ORNAMENTS
CLOTHING

1. On a retarder-moistened surface, basecoat the burgundy areas of clothing with *Burgundy + Paynes Grey (4:1)*. Soften and lighten areas with a dry brush. Dry.

2. Moisten burgundy areas with retarder and shade with *Burgundy + Purple Madder (1:1)*. Dry.

3. On a retarder-moistened surface, basecoat the opposite sides of the clothing with *Ultramarine Blue + Warm White + Paynes Grey (2:2:1)*. Dry.

4. Moisten blue areas with retarder and shade with *Ultramarine Blue + Paynes Grey (2:1)*.

5. Using *Purple Madder + Paynes Grey (1: touch)* and a liner brush, paint the stripes on the burgundy areas and hat. Using the same brush, add *Warm White* dots on the blue sides.

6. Drybrush *Warm White* to highlight lighter areas.

7. Lightly tint with *Aqua* near the shaded areas on the blue sides and with *Permanent Alizarine* on the burgundy sides. Tint with very thin *Paynes Grey* in the deepest shaded areas.

RUFFLED COLLAR AND SOCKS

1. Remove the masking fluid. On a retarder-moistened surface, shade the collar folds and socks with thinned *Ultramarine Blue + Burnt Sienna (1:1)*, then highlight the folds in the collar with *Titanium White*. Dry.

2. Moisten the collar with retarder and tint with *Aqua* near the shaded areas.

3. Using the *step 1 shading color*, float shading on the socks around the shoe opening and below the pants.

SHOES

1. Basecoat the shoes with *Raw Umber + Paynes Grey (1:1)*.

2. Drybrush *Warm White* to highlight.

BOBBLES ON THE CLOTHING, HAT AND SHOES

1. Basecoat the bobbles with *Yellow Oxide + Warm White (1:1)*.

2. Shade the lower side of the bobbles with *Yellow Oxide + Burgundy (1:1)*.

3. Highlight with dots of *Warm White* and tint with *Pale Gold*.

HATBAND

Refer to the bobbles section above for colors and paint the hatband.

RIBBON (hanging from pants pocket)

1. Using a liner brush, paint with *step 3 clothing color*.

2. Shade with thinned *Paynes Grey*, then highlight with *Warm White*.

3. Using a liner brush, paint shadow cast onto the pants with *Ultramarine Blue + Burnt Sienna (2:1)*.

Glue ball to hands

Clowns for Christmas

FACE AND HANDS

1. Moisten the white background with retarder, then shade around the eyes, nose, ears, vertical lines between nose and mouth, and under the mouth and hatband with thinned *Ultramarine Blue + Burnt Sienna (2:1)*. Soften the color with a dry brush. Dry.

2. Paint the irises with *Ultramarine Blue + Warm White (1:1)*. Paint the pupils with *Paynes Grey*; dot a twinkle on the pupils and irises with *Warm White*. Add a touch of *Aqua* to one side of each iris.

3. Using a liner brush and the *step one color*, paint the upper and lower eyelashes, nose and outline the eyes.

4. With *Warm White + Burgundy (1: touch)*, basecoat the round cheeks and tip of the nose. Add a touch more *Burgundy* to this color and paint the lips.

5. Using your flat brush dressed with *Magic Mix* and tipped with *Permanent Alizarine*, float shading on the cheeks, nose and lips. Separate the lips with the *step 1 color.* Highlight lips and nose with *Warm White*.

6. Using a liner brush, paint eyebrows with *Paynes Grey + Raw Umber (1:1)*, then highlight with *Warm White*. Thin the *eyebrow color* with *Flow Medium* and paint a vertical line above and below each eye.

7. On a retarder-moistened surface, tint with *Aqua* near the shaded areas. Dry.

HAND-HELD BALLS

1. Basecoat yellow balls with *Yellow Oxide + Warm White (2:1)*. When dry, overpaint with *Pale Gold*.

2. Basecoat blue balls with *Ultramarine Blue + Paynes Grey (2:1)*. When dry, overpaint with *Blue Iridescent*.

3. Basecoat red balls with *Burgundy*. When dry, overpaint with *Red Iridescent*.

FINISHING

Refer to "Finishing Your Piece" in the General Notes.

OVERHEAD JUGGLING CLOWN: Assemble four balls on a 6-1/2" length of craft wire and glue wire into position. *NOTE: If your bead hole is too large, you may need to glue a piece of wooden toothpick into the hole to secure.*

UNDERHAND JUGGLING CLOWN: Using a large-eyed needle, thread a 6" length of burgundy ribbon through the balls. Glue the balls to secure in place. Position the ribbon ends through the holes in the hands and tie to a knot to secure.

CLOWNS HOLDING BALLS: Glue balls to hands.

FOR ALL: Fold an 8" length of floss or ribbon in half and glue the two ends together. Let dry. Insert glued ends into the hole; glue to secure.

Remaining Patterns on Pages 34-35

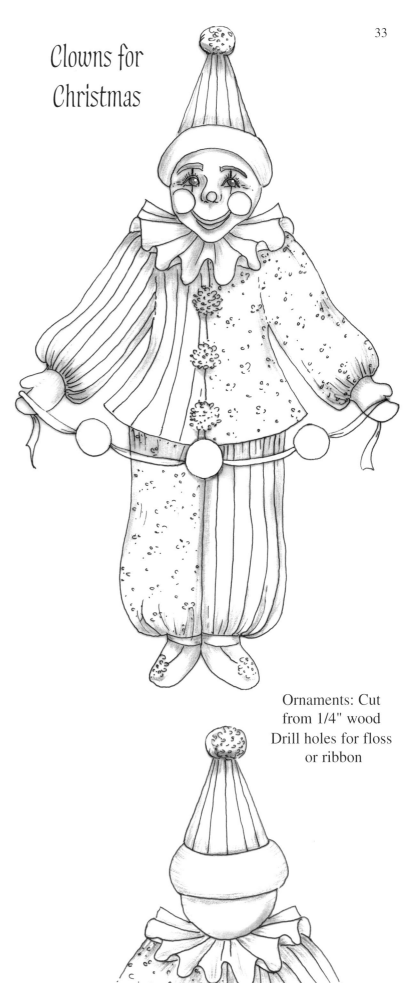

Ornaments: Cut from 1/4" wood
Drill holes for floss or ribbon

Clowns for Christmas
Instructions on Pages 31-33

Glue balls to hands

Ornaments: Cut from 1/4" wood
Drill holes for floss or ribbon, and wire

Bears and Berries

Color Photos on Pages 27 and Back Cover

We have given each of our four children each a hand-painted ornament each year for twenty or so years. They all tell me it is their favorite Christmas gift, and wondering what Mum will come up with this year is one of the highlights of the season.

PALETTE

JO SONJA'S ARTISTS' COLOURS

Antique Green	Raw Umber
Aqua	Red Earth
Brown Earth	Smoked Pearl
French Blue	Storm Blue
Gold Oxide	Teal Green
Napthol Red Light	Titanium White
Naples Yellow Hue	Vermilion
Paynes Grey	Warm White
Purple Madder	Yellow Light
Raw Sienna	

JO SONJA'S BACKGROUND COLOURS

Soft White

ADDITIONAL MATERIALS

Ribbon or braided Pearl thread, 14" for each ornament
Wood glue for securing hangers

BACKGROUND PREPARATION

Please refer to "Basecoating" and "Tracing and Transferring Your Design" at the front of this book.

Basecoat the bear ornaments with two coats of *Soft White + Clear Glaze Medium (2:1)*. Basecoat the wooden labels with two coats of *Smoked Pearl + Clear Glaze Medium (2:1)*. Before transferring the pattern, cut out the outline shape of the ornament and tape the shape to the ornament, then transfer basic design lines. *NOTE: The foliage and berries are much easier freehanded, following the instructions given in this text.*

On the bear pair ornament, basecoat the background area between their heads with thinned *Paynes Grey*. Dry. Float *Paynes Grey* to darken under the heads.

PAINTING YOUR ORNAMENTS

NOTE: The following instructions are used for this entire collection of ornaments.

BEAR FUR AND PAW PAD

1. Basecoat all the fur areas with *Naples Yellow Hue*. Basecoat the paw pad (boy on ornament pair) with *Smoked Pearl + Raw Umber (1: touch)*.

Ornament: Cut
from 1/4" wood

2. On a retarder-moistened surface, paint the fur with *Raw Sienna + Paynes Grey (1: tiny touch)*; use your round brush with slightly open hairs to give a fur-like appearance. Dry.

3. On a retarder-moistened surface, shade the bear's fur and pad with *Raw Sienna + Raw Umber + Brown Earth (2:1: touch)*. Dry.

4. Float the *step 3 color + Paynes Grey (1: touch)* to intensify the shading inside the ears, under the head, and in the deep corners of the arms and legs. Using a liner brush, add darker hairs with the *same color* and lighter hairs with *Warm White*.

5. On a dry background, drybrush *Warm White* highlights on the bear.

EYES

1. Basecoat the eyes with *Gold Oxide,* then paint the pupils with *Paynes Grey + Brown Earth (1: touch)*.

2. Lighten one side of the Gold Oxide eye area with *Yellow Light + Vermilion (1:1)*.

3. Using a liner brush, outline the eyes with very thin *pupil color*. Highlight the eyes with dots of *Warm White*.

NOSE, MOUTH AND PAW STITCHING

1. Using a liner brush, add nose, mouth and stitching with *step 4 shading color (Bear Fur Section)*.

2. Highlight the stitches with touches of *Warm White*.

DRESS

1. Basecoat the bodice with *Smoked Pearl*.

2. On a retarder-moistened surface, shade with very thin *Paynes Grey*. Highlight the moist surface with *Warm White*. Dry. Drybrush *Titanium White* to highlight the bodice.

3. Using a liner brush, add stitching and gather lines, and outline buttons with thinned *Paynes Grey*.

4. On a retarder-moistened surface, tint near the shaded areas with thinned *Aqua*.

5. Basecoat the skirt with *French Blue*; apply two coats to achieve the depth of color.

6. On a retarder-moistened surface, shade the folds with *Paynes Grey*. Dry. Drybrush *Warm White* to highlight.

7. Using a liner brush, paint gathers at the waist with *Paynes Grey*, then use *Warm White* to lighten.

8. On a retarder-moistened surface, tint the skirt with touches of *Aqua*.

WAISTCOAT, DRESS WAISTBAND AND BOWS

1. On a retarder-moistened surface, basecoat the waistcoat with *Red Earth + Napthol Red Light (1:1)*. Use your dry brush to soften the brush strokes and gently pat away color from the lighter areas. Paint the lining with *French Blue*.

(Continued on Page 39)

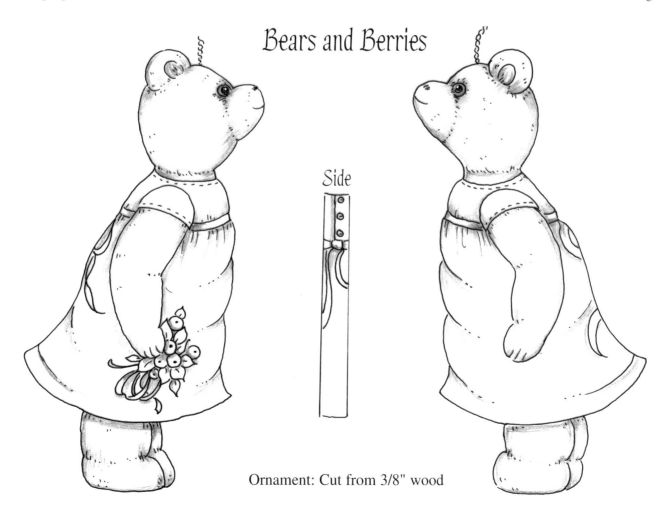

Bears and Berries

Side

Ornament: Cut from 3/8" wood

38

Bears and Berries

Ornaments and Labels:
Cut from 1/4" wood

Wooden Label

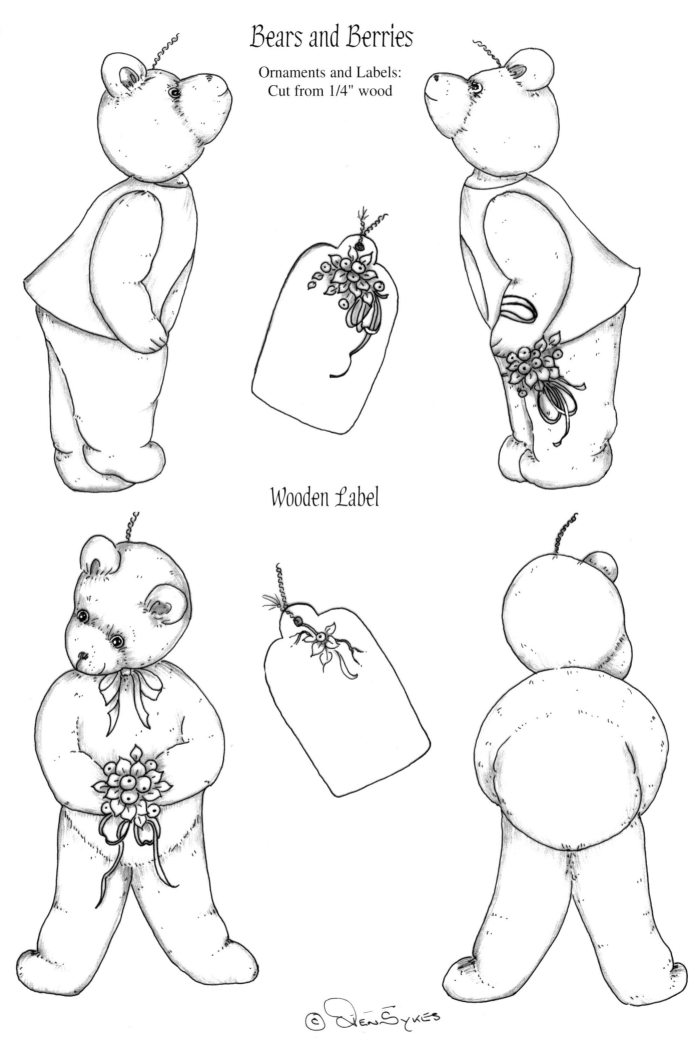

Bears and Berries

(Continued from Page 37)

Dry. Using a liner brush, basecoat waistband and bows with the *red mix*.

2. On a retarder-moistened surface, shade the waistcoat and lining with *Purple Madder*. Dry. Using *Purple Madder*, float shading on the waistband and bows. Dry.

3. Drybrush *Warm White* to highlight the red areas.

4. Using a liner brush, add *Warm White* highlights on edges of waistcoat and bows.

BERRIES

Refer to the color worksheet for instructions.

LEAVES

1. Paint tiny one-stroke leaves with *Antique Green*.

2. Float a little shading at the base of some of the leaves with *Teal Green*.

3. Highlight the veins and some leaf edges with *Warm White + Antique Green (1: tiny touch)*.

RAFFIA RIBBON

1. Using a liner brush, basecoat the raffia with *Raw Sienna + Payne's Grey (1: tiny touch),* then highlight with *Warm White.*

2. With water-thinned *Paynes Grey* and a liner brush, add the shadow lines to the left side of the raffia and dress bows.

WOODEN LABELS

1. On a retarder-moistened surface, tint some areas of the label with thinned *Storm Blue* and other areas with thinned *Raw Sienna*. Soften the brush strokes with a fan brush. Dry.

2. Using a liner brush, paint names and messages to make a wonderful memory. Thinned *Storm Blue + Raw Umber (1: tiny touch)* is a nice dark lettering color. Highlight some of the lettering with touches of *Warm White*.

FINISHING

Refer to "Finishing Your Piece" in the General Notes. Glue one end of ribbon or thread into hole in top of ornament, then thread other end through hole in label and tie.

Christmas Ornament Box

Color Photo on Page 49 and Front Cover

PALETTE

JO SONJA'S ARTISTS' COLOURS

Antique Green	Raw Umber
Aqua	Red Earth
Burnt Sienna	Red Violet
Celadon	Sapphire
French Blue	Skin Tone Base
Gold Oxide	Smoked Pearl
Green Oxide	Storm Blue
Naples Yellow Hue	Teal Green
Nimbus Grey	Titanium White
Paynes Grey	Ultramarine Blue
Permanent Alizarine	Vermilion
Purple Madder	Warm White
Raw Sienna	

JO SONJA'S BACKGROUND COLOURS
Soft White

ADDITIONAL MATERIALS
Art masking fluid
DecoArt Snow-Tex Texturizing Medium
Old toothbrush
Rubbing alcohol, isopropyl
Wooden ball foot trunk, 9" x 6.25" x 5.5"

BACKGROUND PREPARATION

Please refer to "Basecoating" and "Tracing and Transferring Your Design" at the front of the book.

Basecoat the entire box and lid with two coats of *Soft White + Clear Glaze Medium (2:1)*. Dry. Transfer the very basic design lines. Freehand the smaller branches during the painting process.

Carefully apply masking fluid to the cardinals, bell, toys in the toy shop window, Teddy bear near the snowman, and the snowman's hat and scarf.

PAINTING YOUR DESIGN

SKY

1. Moisten the sky area with retarder. Starting at the top edge, paint the sky with a wash of *Storm Blue*; use less color as you near the horizon. Dry.

2. Moisten the sky area with retarder. Shade the top edge with *Paynes Grey* and the horizon with *Red Violet*. Soften these colors with your dry fan brush. Dry.

SNOW AND SNOWMEN

1. Moisten all snow-covered areas and snowmen with retarder and basecoat with *Smoked Pearl + Nimbus Grey (2:1)*. Dry.

2. On a retarder-moistened surface, highlight the lighter areas with *Warm White*. Using your round brush, paint the background hills. Then using a short round brush, stipple this color in the foreground and on the snowmen. Dry.

3. On a retarder-moistened surface, shade with *Ultramarine Blue + Burnt Sienna (1:1)*; soften the color with a dry brush. To add further depth to the shaded areas, use a touch of *Paynes Grey*. On the still moist surface, stipple *Titanium White* to highlight the foreground and snowmen. Dry. Using the *same color*, float highlights on the background hills.

(Continued on Page 40)

Christmas Ornament Box
(Continued from Page 39)

NOTE: Additional Titanium White snow will be added on pathway edges, tree branches, shrubs, fence posts and rooftops after the design has been painted.

4. Basecoat the carrot nose with *Gold Oxide* and shade with *Burnt Sienna*. Drybrush a highlight with *Warm White*.

5. Using a liner brush, add the eyes and buttons with *Raw Umber + Paynes Grey (1:1)*. Highlight with *Warm White* dots. With the same brush, paint mouth with *Ultramarine Blue + Burnt Sienna (1:1)*.

6. Using your round brush and water-thinned *step 3 color*, paint additional shading under the hat brim, scarf, around the eyes, and the cardinal.

7. On a retarder-moistened surface, tint with very thin *Aqua* near the shaded areas.

SNOWMAN'S HAT

1. Basecoat the hat with thinned *Raw Umber + Raw Sienna + Green Oxide (1:1:1)*. Using a liner brush, basecoat the hatband with *Red Earth*.

2. Shade the hat with *Raw Umber + Green Oxide (2:1)*. Darken shaded areas with *Paynes Grey*.

3. Drybrush *Warm White* to highlight the lighter areas. Using a liner brush, apply *same color* on the lighter areas of the hat brim and hatband.

4. On a retarder-moistened surface, lightly tint the shaded areas with *Red Earth*.

SNOWMAN'S SCARF

Refer to the instructions for the scarf on the Snowman Ornament in the "Lynchburg Christmas Collection."

LARGE FIR TREES

1. On a retarder-moistened surface, use your angular brush and *Teal Green* to stipple the foliage as shown on the color worksheet. Dry.

2. Using same brush and color, load the tip with *Antique Green + Warm White (1:1)*. On a retarder-moistened surface, stipple to lighten the branches. On the still moist surface, stipple shading with *Storm Blue + Paynes Grey (1:1)*.

3. Create the appearance of snow with dots of *Titanium White*.

4. Tint the trees with thinned *Celadon*.

SMALL FIR TREES ON THE HORIZON

1. Basecoat the tree shapes with *Antique Green*.

2. Lighten the right side of each tree with *Warm White + Antique Green (2:1)*. Shade the opposite side of the tree and behind overlapping trees with thinned *Paynes Grey*.

3. Using a liner brush, add needles with *Antique Green + Paynes Grey (1:1)* and intensify lighter areas with *Warm White*. Paint tiny dots of *Warm White* to create the appearance of snow.

4. On a retarder-moistened surface, tint with touches of *Celadon*.

SHRUBS

1. On a retarder-moistened surface, stipple *Green Oxide* to form the shape of the shrubbery. Dry.

2. Moisten with retarder and stipple shading with *Green Oxide + Paynes Grey (2:1)*. Add more *Paynes Grey* to this mix for additional depth of shading.

3. Using *step 2 color* and a liner brush, add a few tiny leaves around the exterior to soften the appearance. Using a liner brush, add a few *Red Earth* berries to some of the shrubs for a festive appearance. Using same brush, add dots of snow with *Titanium White*.

PATHWAYS AND STEPS

1. On a retarder-moistened surface, basecoat the pathways and steps with thinned *Raw Sienna + Raw Umber + Paynes Grey (1: touch: touch)*. Using an old toothbrush loaded with rubbing alcohol, fleck the wet surface and quickly dry. Repeat this step two more times.

2. Using the *step 1 color + Paynes Grey (1: touch)*, float shading on the edges of the pathways and steps. Using a liner brush and thickened *Titanium White*, paint the snow at the edge of the pathways. *NOTE: To thicken paint, allow paint to rest on dry palette until a slightly thickened consistency is achieved.*

3. Working on a retarder-moistened surface, tint near the shaded areas with touches of *Aqua*.

4. To add warmth to various areas, touch in *Red Earth*.

FENCES

1. Using *Raw Umber + Nimbus Grey (2:1)* and a liner brush, basecoat the fences and fence posts. Using the *same color*, intensify the shading on left side on each post. Highlight with *Warm White*.

2. Using same brush, apply thickened *Titanium White* snow on upper sides of fencing and fence posts.

TREES, TREE TRUNKS AND DECIDUOUS HEDGEROWS

1. Basecoat these areas with *Raw Umber + Raw Sienna + Green Oxide (2:1:1)*.

2. Shade the trees and trunks with *step 1 color + touch of Paynes Grey*. Highlight with *Warm White*.

3. Using a liner brush, add *Titanium White* snow on branches and hedgerows.

TEDDY BEAR

Refer to Teddy Bear in "Village Toy Shop" for colors and instructions.

For the waistcoat, use the same greens used for green areas of snowman's scarf. Dot *Smoked Pearl + Nimbus Grey (2:1)* for buttons.

CARDINALS

Refer to the Cardinals Ornament in the "Lynchburg Christmas Collection" for colors and instructions. Basecoat the feet with *Raw Umber + Paynes Grey (1:1)* and highlight with *Warm White*.

SCHOOLHOUSE AND TOY SHOP

Refer to the "Village Toy Shop and Schoolhouse" for colors and instructions.

For the Schoolhouse, do not paint foliage, sign, rope on the bell and wood frame above each window.

For the Toy Shop, simplify the toys and tree. Do not add hair on soldier, ribbon on duck and gingerbread on the tree. The front door will be painted the same as the other wood areas. Paint the ornaments on the tree with *Red Earth*.

FAUX ARCHWAY AND NON-DESIGN AREAS

Work each section through to completion, dry, and then continue to another section.

1. On a retarder-moistened surface, paint with *Smoked Pearl + Raw Sienna + Paynes Grey (1:1: touch)*. Fleck the wet surface with rubbing alcohol and quickly dry. *NOTE: If your background has an excess of retarder and is too wet, the paint will bleed back into the areas that the alcohol has cleared. Practice a little before painting the box.*

2. Float the moldings with the *step 1 color + Paynes Grey (1: touch)*.

3. Moisten the faux area with retarder. Tint some areas with touches of very thin *Celadon* and other areas with thinned *Burnt Sienna*. Dry.

4. To give a marbleized appearance to the ball feet, moisten the ball with retarder and let sit for 50 seconds. Using your liner brush and *Burnt Sienna*, paint a thin, irregular line. Very gently pull the brush hairs of a dry fan brush across the line to fragment the line to look like marble. Dry.

FINAL DETAILS

To give a trompe l'oeil effect to the cardinals perched on the archway, use water-thinned *Paynes Grey* to paint a shadow to the left side of his body and beak.

Evaluate all shaded areas and, if needed, darken with *Paynes Grey*.

FINISHING

Refer to "Finishing Your Piece" in the General Instructions.

Using your palette knife, apply *textural medium* on the lower corners of the box and on post caps. Allow to dry, then tint with touches of *Aqua*.

Christmas Ornament Box

Left Side Motif

Reverse for right side

Remaining Patterns on Pages 42-43

Christmas Ornament Box

Instructions on Pages 39-41

Front and Back Motifs

Lid Motif

Village Toy Shop and Schoolhouse

Color Photos on Pages 27, 49 and Back Cover

PALETTE

JO SONJA'S ARTISTS' COLOURS

Aqua	Raw Sienna
Burnt Sienna	Raw Umber
French Blue (Toy Shop)	Red Earth
Green Oxide	Sapphire (Toy Shop)
Naples Yellow Hue	Skin Tone Base (Toy Shop)
Nimbus Grey	Smoked Pearl
Paynes Grey	Storm Blue
Permanent Alizarine (Toy Shop)	Titanium White
Purple Madder	Vermilion (Schoolhouse)
	Warm White

JO SONJA'S BACKGROUND COLOURS
Soft White

JO SONJA'S METALLIC COLOURS
Pale Gold

ADDITIONAL MATERIALS

Art masking fluid
Pearl thread or floss thread, 1 yard
Twigs for apple stems (Bell Ornaments)
Wood glue
Wooden apples, 3/4"
Wooden bells, 1" and 2 1/4"
Wooden books, 1/2" x 5/8" and 1 1/8" x 1 1/2"

BACKGROUND PREPARATION

Please refer to "Basecoating" and "Tracing and Transferring Your Design" at the front of the book.

Basecoat the ornament pieces with two coats of *Soft White + Clear Glaze Medium (2:1)*. Dry.

Before transferring the pattern, cut the design to fit the ornament shape and secure it to the ornament. Gently transfer only the basic design lines.

Apply masking fluid for protection to the following areas:

Village Toy Shop: All the toys in the shop window, Christmas trees, sled and sleigh, and bears in windows and sleigh.

Schoolhouse: Bell, apple, milk can, cat, snowman and snowballs, and star on the tree.

PAINTING YOUR ORNAMENTS

Village Toy Shop

WALLS

1. Using a flat brush dressed with *Magic Mix* and sideloaded with *French Blue*, start under the roof shingles and float each section of the siding panels.

2. Float *Warm White* to lighten the bottom edge of each siding panel.

3. Shade under the roof, and around door and windows with *French Blue + Paynes Grey (1:1)*. Drybrush siding panels with *Warm White*.

4. On a retarder-moistened surface, tint some areas with touches of thinned *Aqua* and other areas with thinned *Raw Sienna*.

ROOF SHINGLES

1. On a retarder-moistened surface, basecoat the roof with *Warm White + Raw Umber + Paynes Grey (2:1: touch)*; use your fan brush to even brush strokes. Dry.

2. Dress a flat brush with *Magic Mix* and sideload with *Raw Umber + Warm White + Paynes Grey (2:1: touch)*. Starting at the ridge of the roof, float shading to separate the layers of shingles. Also float shading to separate the sides of each shingle.

3. Float *Warm White* to lighten some of the shingle bottom edges.

4. Use a liner brush and *step 2 color + a touch of Paynes Grey* to separate shingles and to add cracks to age the shingles; drybrush *Warm White* highlights.

5. On a retarder-moistened surface, tint the roof with *Paynes Grey, Raw Sienna* and *Aqua* to add interest.

WINDOWPANES (shop window and two small ones on the back)

1. On a retarder-moistened surface, paint all the windows with thinned *Raw Umber + Paynes Grey (1:1)*. Even brush strokes diagonally with a fan brush. Dry.

   NOTE: Paint each window separately. The inner window framework will be painted later.

2. At this point, remove the masking from all items in the windows.

WINDOW FRAMES, DOOR FRAME AND SIGNBOARD

NOTE: Paint the various toys and foliage in shop and rear windows before painting the inner window framework.

1. Basecoat the wood areas with *Smoked Pearl + Raw Sienna + Paynes Grey (1:1: touch)*. Dry.

2. Using *Raw Sienna + Raw Umber + Paynes Grey (1:1: touch)*, float shading on the woodwork and the signboard.

3. Using the *step 2 color* and a liner brush, paint the angel and bear designs above the doorway and on the signboard. Using same brush, highlight with *Warm White*. Using *Warm White*, float highlights on the wood frames and signboard. Dry. Complete the highlighting by drybrushing with *Warm White*.

4. On a retarder-moistened surface, tint the signboard and door frame with touches of *Aqua*.

(Continued on Page 46)

Village Toy Shop and Schoolhouse

Village Toy Shop

Ornament: Cut from 1/4" wood
Drill hole in top of bear, book and ornament

Bear Cutout

Optional Cover Design

Book Motif

Add garland above each window

Village Toy Shop

(Continued from Page 44)

5. When you are ready to paint the inner window framework, use a liner brush to basecoat the framework with *Warm White*. Complete these inner frames following the colors given for the window frames. Use a liner brush to shade and highlight.

PATHWAY AND STEP

1. On a retarder-moistened surface, basecoat these areas with *Warm White + Raw Umber + Paynes Grey (2:2: touch)*, then stipple these areas using a dry brush. Dry.

2. Using your flat brush dressed in *Magic Mix* and sideloaded with *Raw Umber + Warm White + Paynes Grey (2:1: touch)*, form the stones in the pathway and the shape of the step. Dry.

3. Drybrush *Warm White* to highlight the stones and step.

4. With *step 2 color + Paynes Grey (1: touch)*, shade the path next to the step and base of the house.

5. On a retarder-moistened surface, tint some areas with thinned *Aqua* and other areas with *Raw Sienna*.

DOOR

1. On the Soft White background, shade the door with *Paynes Grey + Burnt Sienna (1: touch)*, then drybrush *Titanium White* to highlight door panels. Dry.

2. On a retarder-moistened surface, tint the door with touches of thinned *Aqua*. At the door base and under the knob, tint with thinned *Raw Sienna + Raw Umber (1: tiny touch)*. Soften with your filbert brush.

3. Using *step 1 shading color*, basecoat doorknob, then highlight with *Warm White*. Using a liner brush and *same step 1 color*, sharpen the door molding.

SLED AND SLEIGH

1. Basecoat both with *Red Earth*.

2. Using *Purple Madder*, float shading on the sled and sleigh.

3. Using *Warm White*, float highlights on the lighter edges. Dry. Drybrush *Warm White* to highlight larger areas.

4. On a retarder-moistened surface, tint the sled and sleigh with *Permanent Alizarine*.

5. Using a liner brush, paint the sleigh runners and sled rope handle with *Raw Umber + Paynes Grey (1:1)*. Using same brush, highlight with *Warm White*.

6. With a liner brush and very thin *Paynes Grey*, paint the shadows behind the sleigh runners.

CHRISTMAS TREES

1. On a retarder-moistened surface, paint *Green Oxide* branches. Use your round brush and pull strokes to create a streaked appearance. Dry.

2. Using *Green Oxide + Paynes Grey (2:1)*, float shading under the branches.

3. Lighten the upper side of the branches with strokes of *Warm White + Green Oxide (1: touch)*, using more *Warm White* as you near the tree center.

4. Using your liner brush and the *shading color*, enhance the tree by painting tiny needles. Using the same method, highlight needles with *Warm White*. Float shading on the tree in the window next to the frame with *Paynes Grey*.

5. On a retarder-moistened surface, tint the lower area of the tree with *Aqua*.

GARLANDS AND WREATHS

1. Paint tiny one-stroke leaves with *Green Oxide*. Using *Green Oxide + Paynes Grey (2:1)*, float shading on some of the leaves.

2. Using a liner brush, apply *Warm White* to highlight veins and leaf edges (not all the leaves).

3. Basecoat the tiny berries with *Naples Yellow Hue*, then overpaint with *Red Earth*. Dot *Paynes Grey* seeds in some of the berries. Highlight some of the berries with a dot of *Warm White*.

4. Using a liner brush and *Raw Umber + Green Oxide (2:1)*, add twigs around the garlands. Highlight with touches of *Warm White*.

5. Using liner brush, basecoat the ribbon on the door wreath with *Red Earth*, then highlight with *Warm White*.

GINGERBREAD MEN AND BEARS (including bear cutout)

1. Roll away masked areas. Basecoat all the bears and gingerbread men with *Naples Yellow Hue*.

2. On a retarder-moistened surface, paint all with *Raw Sienna*, using more color in the shaded areas. Use a dry brush to soften the color and lighten areas. Dry.

3. Shade with *Raw Sienna + Burnt Sienna + Raw Umber (1: touch: touch)*. Using a liner brush and *same color*, paint faces and buttons on gingerbread men. Using liner brush and *same color*, paint claws and a few fur lines on bear cutout.

4. Highlight with *Warm White*; using the *same color*, drybrush large areas.

5. Dot eyes and noses, and paint mouths with *Raw Umber + Paynes Grey (1:1)*; highlight eyes and nose with *Warm White*.

DOLL

1. Basecoat the hat and coat with *Sapphire + Warm White (1:1)*. Basecoat collar with *Warm White*.

2. Shade hat, coat and collar with *Sapphire + Paynes Grey (1:1)*.

3. Highlight hat and coat with *Warm White*.

4. Using liner brush, dot *Sapphire + Paynes Grey (1:1)* buttons on front of the coat.

5. Basecoat the face with *Skin Tone Base*. Float shading around the hairline and eye sockets with thinned *Burnt Sienna*.

6. Blush the cheeks and line the mouth with *Red Earth + Warm White (1: touch)*.

7. Dot the eyes with *Sapphire* and highlight with *Warm White* dots. Using a liner brush, paint the nose and eyebrows, and outline eyes with very thin *Burnt Sienna*. Highlight the nose and cheeks with *Warm White*.

8. Basecoat the hair with *Naples Yellow Hue*. Shade the hair with *Raw Sienna*, then add *Warm White* dots to highlight.

YELLOW CHICK

1. Basecoat with *Naples Yellow Hue* and shade with thinned *Raw Sienna*. Drybrush highlights with *Warm White*.

2. Dot the eye with *Raw Umber + Paynes Grey (1:1),* then highlight with a dot of *Warm White*.

3. Using a liner brush, paint the beak with *Raw Sienna*. With the same brush, paint lines to shade next to the beak with *Raw Sienna + Burnt Sienna (1: touch)*. Highlight beak with *Warm White*.

4. Using *doll coat colors,* freehand the ribbons above chick and on bear cutout.

TOY SOLDIER

1. Basecoat the face with *Skin Tone Base*. Float shading around the hairline and eye sockets with thinned *Burnt Sienna*.

2. Blush the cheeks with *Red Earth + Warm White (1: touch)*.

3. Dot the eyes and nose with *Paynes Grey*, then highlight eyes with *Warm White* dots.

4. Using a liner brush, paint the mouth and eyebrows with *Paynes Grey*.

5. Paint the hair with thinned *Raw Umber + Paynes Grey (1:1)*.

6. Basecoat the coat with *French Blue*, then shade with *French Blue + Paynes Grey (1:1)*. Shade and separate coat panels with *French Blue + Paynes Grey (1:1)*.

7. Basecoat the hat and trousers with *Red Earth + Purple Madder (1:1)*. Shade with *Purple Madder*; highlight hat with *Warm White*.

8. Using a liner brush, add epaulets and buttons with *Naples Yellow Hue*.

HOBBY HORSE

1. Basecoat the head and ears with *Nimbus Grey + Warm White (1:1)*.

2. Shade with strokes of *Nimbus Grey + Paynes Grey (1: touch)*.

3. Dot the eye with *Raw Umber + Paynes Grey (1:1)*, then highlight with a tiny dot of *Warm White*.

4. Tint inside each ear with *Red Earth + Warm White (1: touch)*.

5. Paint the harness and pole with *Raw Sienna + Raw Umber (2:1)*. Shade edge with the *same color + a touch of Paynes Grey*. Highlight with *Warm White*. Using a liner brush, add rivets on the harness with *Raw Umber + Paynes Gray (1:1)*; highlight with *Warm White* dots.

6. Using a liner brush, add the mane with *Naples Yellow Hue*. Shade with strokes of *Raw Sienna* and highlight with strokes of *Warm White*.

BOAT

1. On a retarder-moistened surface, basecoat the hull with *Paynes Grey + Storm Blue (1:1)*. Use more color in the shaded areas.

2. On the still moist surface, shade the Soft White sails with thinned *Paynes Grey*. Dry.

3. Basecoat the deck of the boat with *Raw Umber + Green Oxide (1: touch)*. Shade by adding a touch of *Paynes Grey* to this color.

4. Using a liner brush, basecoat the mast and booms with *Raw Umber + Paynes Grey (1:1)*; highlight with *Warm White*.

5. Using a liner brush, paint a *Red Earth* band around the boat hull.

6. Drybrush *Warm White* to highlight the hull. Use *Titanium White* to highlight the sails.

DOLLHOUSE

1. Basecoat the roof and door with thinned *Red Earth*.

2. Using your flat brush dressed with *Magic Mix* and side-loaded with *Red Earth*, float the tile separations on roof. Dry.

3. Drybrush *Warm White* highlights on roof and door.

4. Shade the roof near the edge of the shop window with *Paynes Grey*.

5. Shade the Soft White walls with thinned *Storm Blue + Raw Umber (1: touch)*. Using a liner brush, paint details around the window and door, and basecoat the doorknob the *same thinned color*. Highlight doorknob with a dot of *Warm White*.

6. Basecoat the window in the same manner as the larger windows. Paint the linework with *Warm White*.

BOOK

1. Float shading on the Soft White book cover and spine edges with thinned *Storm Blue + Raw Umber (1: touch)*.

2. Paint the pages with *Raw Sienna*, then shade the edges with thinned *Paynes Grey*. On a retarder-moistened surface, tint the page edges with *Pale Gold*.

3. Refer to bear instructions to complete the book cover. Paint ribbon same as on door wreath.

LETTERING

1. Using a liner brush, paint the lettering on the signboard and book spine with thinned *Storm Blue + Raw Umber (1: touch)*.

2. Highlight letters on signboard with *Warm White*.

Schoolhouse

WALLS, CHIMNEY, STEPS, PATHWAY AND DOOR FRAME

1. Basecoat the walls, chimney, steps and pathway with *Smoked Pearl + Raw Sienna + Paynes Grey (3:1: touch)*. Since this is a pale color, float over the door, windows and sign. Dry.

(Continued on Page 48)

Schoolhouse

(Continued from Page 47)

2. Basecoat the timbered beams and door frame with retarder-thinned *Raw Umber + Warm White + Paynes Grey (2:1: touch)*. Using a liner brush and the *same color*, add the wood graining.

3. You'll find it easier to freehand the wall stones rather than following a pattern. Using your flat brush dressed with *Magic Mix* and sideloaded with *Warm White + Raw Umber + Paynes Grey (2:1: touch)*, float shading on one side of each wall and chimney stone. When complete, turn your work upside-down and complete the opposite side. Using this *same color*, stipple the pathway and steps.

4. Shade some of the stone edges and the steps by adding a touch more *Paynes Grey* to the *step 4 mix*.

5. Drybrush *Warm White* to highlight timbered beams, door frame, some stones and doorsteps.

6. On a retarder-moistened surface, tint with thinned *Aqua* on some wall areas and *Raw Sienna* on others. Dry and remove masking.

ROOF

Refer to the instructions given for the "Village Toy Shop" roof.

WINDOWPANES

1. On a retarder-moistened surface, paint the window area with thin *Paynes Grey + Raw Umber (1: touch)*. Use a fan brush with diagonal strokes to even out the brush strokes. Dry.

2. Moisten the front windows with retarder and tint the outer areas with *Aqua* and the inner edges with thinned *Vermilion*. Soften these colors with a dry brush. Repeat for the rear window, tinting edges with *Vermilion* and center with *Aqua*.

GABLES, SIGNBOARD, DOOR AND WINDOW FRAMES

1. On a retarder-moistened surface (except for the window frame), basecoat with *Red Earth + Raw Umber (2:1)*. Dry. Basecoat the window frames with your round or liner brush.

2. Shade with *Red Earth + Raw Umber (1:1)* and highlight with *Warm White*.

3. Shade under gables, around windows, chimney next to the roof and next to the door frame with thinned *Paynes Grey*.

LETTERING ON SIGNBOARD

1. With your liner brush and the *wall basecoat color*, paint the lettering or your child's/grandchild's name (i.e. Katie's School). This makes for a happy memory.

2. Using a liner brush, shadow the letters with *Paynes Grey*. Highlight, if needed, with *Warm White*.

BELL, DOORKNOB, MILK CAN AND BELL ROPE CLEAT

1. Basecoat with *Nimbus Grey* and shade with *Storm Blue + Paynes Grey (1:1)*. Use the *shading color* to outline the milk can and paint the lettering.

2. Highlight with *Warm White* and tint with touches of *Aqua*.

CAT

1. Basecoat with *Naples Yellow Hue*.

2. On a retarder-moistened surface, overpaint the entire cat with *Raw Sienna*. Soften color in the lighter areas. Dry.

3. Shade the cat's body with *Raw Sienna + Raw Umber (1: touch)*; add markings using a liner brush and *same color*. Highlight with *Warm White*.

4. Dot the eye with *step 3 color + Paynes Grey (1: touch)*.

5. Add a tint of *Red Earth*.

ROPE FROM THE BELL

1. Using a liner brush, basecoat with the *wall basecoat color*, then add "S" strokes to shade the twists with the *timbered beam color*.

2. Highlight with touches of *Warm White*.

CHRISTMAS TREE

Refer to the instructions given in the "Village Toy Shop" section.

CHRISTMAS TREE TRUNK AND BENCH UNDER FRONT WINDOW

1. Basecoat with *Raw Umber + Green Oxide (2:1)*.

2. Shade with *step 1 color + Paynes Grey (1: touch)*.

3. Highlight with *Warm White*.

4. Stipple a tint of *Green Oxide* on tree trunk.

FOLIAGE

Refer to the instructions given in the "Village Toy Shop" section.

APPLES

1. Basecoat each apple with *Naples Yellow Hue*.

2. Using *Red Earth,* float a "C" stroke on one side of each apple. When dry, turn your work upside-down and complete each apple with another "C" stroke.

3. Shade the base of the apples with *Red Earth + Purple Madder (1:1)*.

4. Using a liner brush, paint the stems with *Raw Umber + Green Oxide (1: touch)*.

5. Highlight apples and stems with *Warm White*.

CANDLES

1. Using a liner brush and *Naples Yellow Hue + Warm White (1:1)*, basecoat each candle.

2. Shade the base of the candles with *Raw Sienna*, then drybrush a *Warm White* highlight.

3. Shade behind the candles with thinned *Paynes Grey*.

4. Using a liner brush, add the candlewick and holder with *Paynes Grey + Burnt Sienna (1: touch)*; highlight holder with *Warm White*.

STAR ON THE TREETOP

1. Basecoat with *Naples Yellow Hue*.

2. Shade the low points of the star with very thin *Vermilion*.

(Continued on Page 50)

Village Toy Shop and
Schoolhouse
Pages 44-48 & 50-51

Christmas
Ornament Box
Pages 39-43

Schoolhouse

(Continued from Page 48)

3. Highlight the top of the star with *Warm White*.

SNOWMAN AND SNOWBALLS

1. On a retarder-moistened surface, stipple with *Smoked Pearl + Nimbus Grey (2:1)*. Dry.

2. On a retarder-moistened surface, shade with *Nimbus Grey + Paynes Grey (1: touch)*.

3. On a slightly moist surface, stipple highlights first with *Warm White*, then with *Titanium White*. Dry.

4. Basecoat the nose with *Raw Sienna + Red Earth (1: touch)*. Shade the nose with *Red Earth + Raw Umber (1: touch)*. Drybrush a highlight with *Warm White*.

5. Dot the eyes and mouth with *Paynes Grey + Raw Umber (1: touch)*. Highlight with dots of *Warm White*.

6. Basecoat the scarf with *Red Earth*. Float shading with *Red Earth + Purple Madder (1:1)*. Using a liner brush, paint the knitted rows with the *shading color*. Highlight with

Warm White. Paint the fringe with the *basecoat color* and *shading color*.

7. On a retarder-moistened surface, tint additional shading on snowman with *Paynes Grey* in some areas and in other areas with *Aqua*.

8. Using a round brush and water-thinned *Paynes Grey*, add shadows on the wall behind the rope, cat, milk can, apple, star and snowman.

SNOW AROUND AND ON THE SCHOOLHOUSE

On a retarder-moistened surface, stipple lightly with *Warm White*, followed by *Titanium White*. Just as with the snowman, if you lose shading variations, tint with very thin *Paynes Grey* and near shaded areas with *Aqua*.

BOOK

Refer to the instructions for the book in the "Village Toy Shop." Replace the bear design with an apple design.

BELL

1. Refer to the bell instructions in this section. Use same colors for flat bottom of bell.

Schoolhouse

Book Motif

Side

Ornaments: Cut from 1/4" wood. Drill hole in top of book and ornament.

2. Basecoat handle with *Red Earth + Raw Umber (2:1)* and highlight with *Warm White*.

Bell Ornaments

WOODEN APPLES

1. Basecoat *Naples Yellow Hue* and streak with *Red Earth*.

2. In stem area, paint and blend in *Green Oxide*.

3. Using a liner brush, add details to bottom with *Paynes Grey*.

BELL

1. Refer to the bell instructions in this section. Basecoat the handle with thinned *Raw Umber + Raw Sienna (1:1)*. Paint the base of the handle with *Pale Gold*.

2. Refer to "Village Toy Shop" for garland.

BOOKS

1. Refer to "Village Toy Shop" ornament to paint the books, wreath and lettering.

2. Refer to "Schoolhouse" to paint the apples. Paint the leaf with thinned *Green Oxide*.

FINISHING

Refer to "Finishing Your Piece" in the General Notes.

VILLAGE TOY SHOP AND SCHOOLHOUSE: Glue a 2" strand of thread to each of the books, bear and bell. Cut three 6" strands of thread and braid. When you have braided three-fourths of the length, add the thread for the small wooden items and continue braiding until complete. Fold over and glue the two ends. Roll ends between your fingertips to roll the threads together. Dry. Add glue into top hole and place braided thread into hole. Dry.

BELL ORNAMENTS: Glue the twig in the apple. Use thread to attach both ends of each ornament. Also glue a small piece of thread to the bottom of each book.

Village Toy Shop and Schoolhouse

Bell Ornaments

Book Motifs

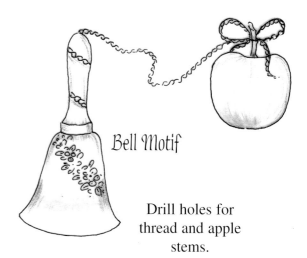

Bell Motif

Drill holes for thread and apple stems.

Village Toy Shop and
Schoolhouse
Pages 44-48 & 50-51

Bears and
Berries
Pages 36-39

ISBN 1-58891-079-2

7 16866 79059 6

Made in the USA